The Earth Atlas

Illustrated by Richard Bonson

Written by Susanna van Rose

Penguin Random House

DK LONDON	**DK INDIA**
Senior Editor	**Desk Editor**
Fleur Star	Saumya Agarwal
Project Art Editor	**Managing Editor**
Gregory McCarthy	Saloni Singh
US Editor	**Managing Art Editor**
Jennette ElNaggar	Govind Mittal
Managing Editor	**Senior Picture Researcher**
Lindsay Kent	Sumedha Chopra
Managing Art Editor	**DTP Designers**
Michelle Baxter	Satish Gaur, Rakesh Kumar
Production Editor	Nityanand Kumar
Robert Dunn	**Senior Jacket Designer**
Senior Production Controller	Suhita Dharamjit
Rachel Ng	**Senior Jackets Coordinator**
Jacket Design Development Manager	Priyanka Sharma Saddi
Sophia MTT	
Publisher	
Andrew Macintyre	
Art Director	
Karen Self	
Publishing Director	
Jonathan Metcalf	

Consultant
Professor Dorrik Stow FRSE

FIRST EDITION
Senior Art Editor Martyn Foote
Project Editors Laura Buller and Fran Jones
Art Editor Dorian Spencer Davies
Production Shelagh Gibson
Managing Editor Susan Peach
Managing Art Editor Jacquie Gulliver
Consultant Keith Lye
Additional illustrations Kuo Kang Chen,
Fiona Bell Currie, and Andrew Robinson.
Picture research Joanna Thomas and Clive Webster.

This American Edition, 2022
First American Edition, 1994
Published in the United States by DK Publishing
1745 Broadway, 20th Floor, New York, NY 10019

Copyright © 1994, 2022 Dorling Kindersley Limited
DK, a Division of Penguin Random House LLC
22 23 24 25 26 10 9 8 7 6 5 4 3 2 1
001–333067–Nov/2022

A catalog record for this book is available from the Library of Congress.
ISBN 978-0-7440-6505-3

Printed and bound in Malaysia

For the curious
www.dk.com

This book was made with Forest
Stewardship Council™ certified paper –
one small step in DK's commitment to
a sustainable future. For more information
go to www.dk.com/our-green-pledge

CONTENTS

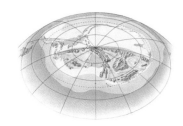

Putting the Earth in a Book

How CAN the entire Earth be squeezed between the pages of a book? In order to explain how the Earth looks, this book uses several different ways to show the round Earth on flat paper. The rocky outer surface that humans and animals live on is just a small part of the whole Earth. To understand the forces that have shaped and changed its surface, the illustrations in this book sometimes cut through Earth's layers right down to its center. In addition, maps, photographs, and diagrams help show the huge variety of Earth's landscapes and explain how they were created. Together, the elements in this book show how the Earth really works.

The Americas   *Africa and Europe*   *East Asia and Oceania*   *The Pacific Rim*

Four faces of the Earth
Above are four different globe views of the Earth, each focusing on a different area. One of these four faces appears on most pages of the book, to give an idea of the location of the main illustration for that page.

A page explained
The double page below shows how the information is presented in this book. An introduction gives an outline of the most important facts and ideas. Most pages feature an illustration of a particular place on Earth, chosen to represent a particular geographical feature. Details are explained by smaller illustrations.

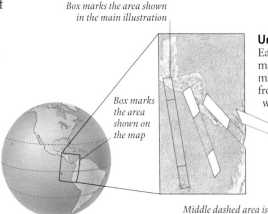

Box marks the area shown in the main illustration

Box marks the area shown on the map

Understanding the maps
Each globe view of the Earth includes a box marking the area shown on a more detailed map. A section of the Earth's surface is cut from this map, then lifted out and laid down with the sky on top. This section is featured in the main illustration. Areas not shown are marked with a dashed line.

Middle dashed area is left out of the illustration

Illustration features these two areas from the map

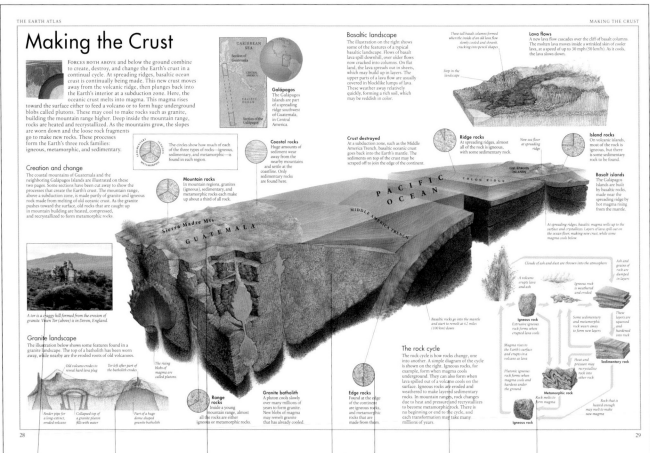

Making the Crust

FORCES BOTH ABOVE and below the ground combine to create, destroy, and change the Earth's crust in a continual cycle. At spreading ridges, basaltic ocean crust is continually being made. This new crust moves away from the volcanic ridge, then plunges back into the Earth's interior at a subduction zone. Here, the oceanic crust melts into magma. This magma rises toward the surface either to feed a volcano or to form huge underground blobs called plutons. These may cool to make rocks such as granite, building the mountain range higher. Deep inside the mountain range, rocks are heated and recrystallized. As the mountains grow, the slopes are worn down and the loose rock fragments go to make new rocks. These processes form the Earth's three rock families: igneous, metamorphic, and sedimentary.

Galápagos
The Galápagos Islands are part of a spreading ridge southwest of Guatemala, in Central America.

Basaltic landscape
The illustration on the right shows some of the features of a typical basaltic landscape. Flows of basalt lava spill downhill, over older flows now cracked into columns. On flat land, the lava spreads out in sheets, which may build up in layers. The upper parts of a lava flow are usually covered in blocklike lumps of lava. These weather away relatively quickly, forming a rich soil, which may be reddish in color.

Lava flows
A new lava flow cascades over the cliff of basalt columns. The molten lava moves inside a wrinkled skin of cooler lava, at a speed of up to 30 mph (50 km/h). As it cools, the lava slows down.

These tall basalt columns formed when the inside of an old lava flow slowly cooled and shrank, cracking into pencil shapes

Step in the landscape

Creation and change
The coastal mountains of Guatemala and the neighboring Galápagos Islands are illustrated on these two pages. Some sections have been cut away to show the processes that create the Earth's crust. The mountain range, above a subduction zone, is made partly of granite and igneous rock made from melting of old oceanic crust. As the granite pushes toward the surface, old rocks that are caught up in mountain building are heated, compressed, and recrystallized to form metamorphic rocks.

The circles show how much of each of the three types of rocks—igneous, sedimentary, and metamorphic—is found in each region.

Coastal rocks
Huge amounts of sediment wear away from the nearby mountains and settle at the coastline. Only sedimentary rocks are found here.

Crust destroyed
At a subduction zone, such as the Middle America Trench, basaltic oceanic crust goes back into the Earth's mantle. The sediments on top of the crust may be scraped off to join the edge of the continent.

Ridge rocks
At spreading ridges, almost all of the rock is igneous, with some sedimentary rock.

New sea floor at spreading ridge

Island rocks
On volcanic islands, most of the rock is igneous, but there is some sedimentary rock to be found.

Mountain rocks
In mountain regions, granites (igneous), sedimentary, and metamorphic rocks each make up about a third of all rock.

Basalt islands
The Galápagos Islands are built by basaltic rocks, made near the spreading ridge by hot magma rising from the mantle.

Sierra Madre Mts
GUATEMALA
PACIFIC OCEAN
MIDDLE AMERICA TRENCH
COLON RIDGE
GALÁPAGOS ISLANDS

At spreading ridges, basaltic magma wells up to the surface and crystallizes. Layers of lava spill out on the ocean floor, making new crust, while some magma cools below.

A tor is a craggy hill formed from the erosion of granite. Vixen Tor (above) is in Devon, England.

Basaltic rocks go into the mantle and start to remelt at 62 miles (100 km) down

Clouds of ash and dust are thrown into the atmosphere

Ash and grains of rock are dumped in layers

A volcano erupts lava and ash

Igneous rock
Extrusive igneous rock forms when erupted lava cools

Igneous rock is weathered and eroded

Some sedimentary and metamorphic rock wears away to form new layers

These layers are squeezed and hardened into rock

Granite landscape
The illustration below shows some features found in a granite landscape. The top of a batholith has been worn away, while nearby are the eroded roots of old volcanoes.

Old volcano erodes to reveal hard lava plug

Top left after part of the batholith erodes

The rising blobs of magma are called plutons

The rock cycle
The rock cycle is how rocks change, one into another. A simple diagram of the cycle is shown on the right. Igneous rocks, for example, form when magma cools underground. They can also form when lava spilled out of a volcano cools on the surface. Igneous rocks are eroded and weathered to make layered sedimentary rocks. In mountain ranges, rock changes due to heat and pressure and recrystallizes to become metamorphic rock. There is no beginning or end to the cycle, and each transformation may take many millions of years.

Magma rises to the Earth's surface and erupts in a volcano or lava

Plutonic igneous rock forms when magma cools and hardens under the ground

Heat and pressure may recrystallize rock into other rock

Sedimentary rock

Feeder pipe for a long-extinct, eroded volcano

Collapsed top of a granite pluton fills with water

Part of a huge dome-shaped granite batholith

Range rocks
Inside a young mountain range, almost all the rocks are either igneous or metamorphic rocks.

Granite batholith
A pluton cools slowly over many millions of years to form granite. New blobs of magma may remelt granite that has already cooled.

Edge rocks
Found at the edge of the continent are igneous rocks, metamorphic rocks that are made from them.

Rock melts to form magma

Metamorphic rock

Igneous rock

Rock that is heated enough may melt to make new magma

28   29

Photographs
These show what landscapes look like when they are made of the rocks, or formed by the geological process, described on the double page.

Place names help locate the illustrations.

Small illustrations show details of landscapes related to the main illustration.

Main illustrations
Different colors are used to show the different kinds of rocks that occur in the places featured in the main illustrations.

This detail shows the rock types found in this part of the Earth

Captions
These work closely with the illustrations to present facts and information.

Charts and diagrams
Ideas that relate to the main illustration are often explained by charts and diagrams. Some step-by-step diagrams show how a landscape was formed.

Cutting up mountains

Some of the main illustrations feature huge chunks of the Earth. This one, representing the Himalayas and Tibet, shows a section of the Earth that is really hundreds of miles long.

The section of the Earth featured in the illustration is boxed on the globe view

The section is cut out, lifted, and then laid flat

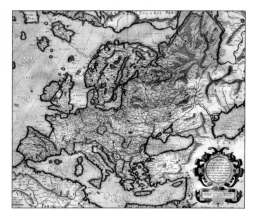

Ancient maps (right) were based as much on imagination as on fact. Today, mapmakers compare their maps with satellite photographs (above).

Once the illustration is laid flat, it is easier to understand.

A closer look

A piece of the main illustration is often pulled out and made bigger so that details are easier to see. This section, for example, shows what the rocks inside the mountains look like.

This block has been cut out of the main artwork and made larger

Mapping the Earth

Although the nearly round Earth is most accurately represented as a globe, flat maps provide an almost complete picture of a large area. The maps in this book are used to show specific areas featured in the illustrations. Others show the major mountain ranges, deserts, and frozen regions on Earth.

Below the surface

The pulled-out blocks of the illustration show us not only the land surface but also what is going on in the layers underneath. Sometimes this is important in helping to understand the surface landscape and rocks.

These dashed line areas show sections that are left out

This is the most distant section

This is a section taken from the middle of the glacier

This is the end, or snout section of the glacier

Cutouts

This illustration of the Athabasca glacier in Canada shows inside and underneath the glacier—views it is not normally possible to see. The inside of the glacier is shown in cuts through the illustration, which are pulled apart to give a better view. In one section of the illustration, the whole glacier is removed, along with all the boulders and rock fragments trapped in the ice, to show the rocky surface below.

Times change

Landscape is always changing, but usually very slowly. Sometimes change happens rapidly—the volcanic eruption at Mount St. Helens blew the side of the mountain away in only hours (right). Other changes have happened slowly, over tens of thousands of years. Illustrations such as the sequence below are used to show these changes.

This is Mount St. Helens before its eruption.

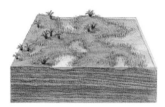

100 million years ago

This is a landscape as it might have looked 100 million years ago. Dinosaurs roamed over swamps and left their footprints in the wet sand.

40 million years ago

This is the same place 40 million years later. The dinosaurs are now extinct, their footprints long since buried. The land has sunk and is under a shallow, young sea.

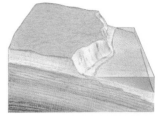

Today

Today, the sea is gone, and dry land is left behind. The muddy ooze that was on the seabed has hardened into chalk, which is being eroded into steep cliffs.

After the eruption, there is a large hole where the mountain summit once was.

Earth Is Unique

AMONG THE PLANETS of the solar system, Earth is unique in many ways. Its atmosphere contains oxygen, which lets it support life. Oxygen makes up a critical one-fifth of the Earth's atmosphere—if there were slightly more, plants would spontaneously catch fire. Water covers most of the Earth's surface, keeping temperatures moderate and releasing essential water vapor into the atmosphere. Inside, restless currents create a magnetic field that shields the Earth from space radiation. Other internal movements cause the surface to slowly churn over so that the crust is constantly renewing or reshaping itself.

The inner Earth

Earth's surface rocks are made mostly of the chemical elements oxygen and silicon, along with some metals. Beneath this is a thick layer of heavier rock called the mantle. This encloses the inner and outer cores. The solid metal inner core is the densest part of the Earth. The liquid outer core is always moving, causing a constantly changing magnetic field to envelop the planet.

Crust
The solid, rocky surface that we live on is called the crust. It is thickest under the continents, and thinnest below the oceans.

Earth imagined
Ancient people had no way of knowing about the inner Earth. The painting below illustrates the world system of the Babylonians. The Earth is a round, hollow mountain resting on water. The sky, with fixed stars, meteors, and planets, forms a hollow chamber. The sun rises each day through a door in the east and sets through a door in the west.

Lithosphere and asthenosphere
The outermost 62 miles (100 km) of the mantle is firmly attached to the Earth's outer crust. Together, these make up the lithosphere. Below the lithosphere is a layer of hotter, softer rock another 62 miles (100 km) thick. This is called the asthenosphere.

Mantle
Making up about nine-tenths of the total bulk of the Earth, the mantle is a thick shell of hot, rocky silicate minerals. Although the mantle is solid, it does slowly circulate over millions of years.

Green planet
Plants living on the land surface color the continents green. Plants take in carbon dioxide from the atmosphere and use it to make chlorophyll. In the process, they give out oxygen, used by animals and people.

Land planet
Earth's land areas cover just over a quarter of its surface, where the continents rise above sea level.

Air planet
The mixture of gases and water vapor wrapped around the Earth is its atmosphere. Its swirling white clouds are constantly on the move.

Water planet
Nearly three-quarters of the Earth's surface is covered by water, most of it within its vast oceans.

Outer core
Surrounding the solid inner core is the liquid outer core. Its molten iron and nickel metals are at the slightly cooler temperature of 9,932°F (5,500°C) and are under less pressure than the inner core. The movement of this hot liquid generates the Earth's magnetic field.

Inner core
At the heart of the planet is its inner core, made of iron and nickel. The temperature is so high here—10,832°F (6,000°C)—that these metals should be molten liquid, but the immense pressure compresses them into solids.

Summer solstice
On June 21, the tilt of the Earth's axis means the strongest and most direct light from the sun is in the northern hemisphere. There is a full 24 hours of daylight in the Arctic Circle, and the northern hemisphere has its longest day.

Northern hemisphere spring

Spring equinox
At the spring equinox on March 21, the sun is directly overhead at the equator. Days and nights have equal length all over the Earth.

Northern hemisphere summer

Note: this diagram is not to scale.

Northern hemisphere winter

Autumnal equinox
As in the spring equinox, the sun is directly overhead at the equator during the autumnal equinox. Day and night are once again the same length in both hemispheres.

Northern hemisphere fall

Winter solstice
On December 21, the tilt of the Earth means the sun's direct light and heat strike south of the equator. This is the longest day in the southern hemisphere.

The Earth's orbit
Earth travels around the sun, taking one year to make a complete round trip. This pathway is called its orbit. Earth's orbit is not quite circular but slightly oval. As it makes its orbit, Earth is also spinning around on its axis. Each complete spin takes 24 hours. When light from the sun illuminates half of the globe, this region has day while the dark half has night. Our seasons (above) are also a result of the Earth's orbit and rotation.

A beautiful result of the Earth's magnetism is an aurora. The Earth's magnetic poles attract charged particles in the atmosphere, which radiate colored light.

The Earth's plates
The Earth's lithosphere is broken into fewer than a dozen large and many smaller plates. These move slowly and steadily. Everything carried on them moves, too—from huge continents to entire oceans.

Hydrosphere
The hydrosphere includes the Earth's oceans, lakes, rivers, underground water, and snow and ice. The hydrosphere covers the oceanic crust almost totally, to an average depth of 3 miles (5 km).

Atmosphere
The atmosphere is at least 620 miles (1,000 km) thick. The atmosphere is densest in the lowest 6 miles (10 km), the troposphere. Above this is the stratosphere, where the atmosphere is thinner because it contains fewer molecules.

Upper part of the mantle and the crust forms the lithosphere

A gas called ozone shields the Earth from some of the sun's rays

Thick continental crust

Thin oceanic crust

Hydrosphere

The outer Earth
The solid rocky surface of the Earth is always changing. Here, the Earth's rocks meet—and interact—with the hydrosphere and the atmosphere. The rocks react both chemically and physically with these layers. Moving air and water and temperature changes break down the rocks physically. Oxygen from the atmosphere reacts with silicates in the rocks to change them chemically, making new rocky minerals.

Troposphere

Stratosphere

Mesosphere

Thermosphere

Exosphere and magnetosphere

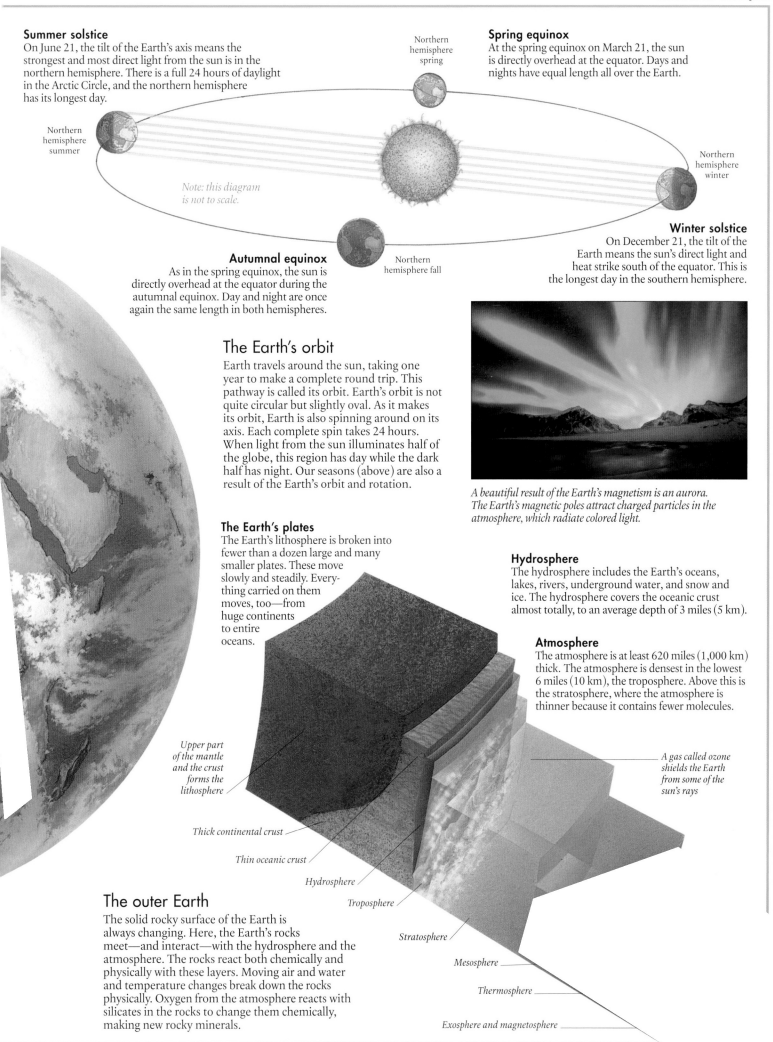

Bombardment from Space

THE EARLY HISTORY OF THE EARTH is shrouded in mystery. But the events of this first billion years—since the Earth formed around 4.5 billion years ago—set the scene for the planet of today. During that time, the Earth evolved out of a cloud of dust to a cooling, crusted planet wrapped in an envelope of gases. Its first rocky skin was ripped apart by the impact of huge meteorites. This bombardment of Earth and the other planets went on while the crust grew thick enough to withstand the impact and cool enough for rainwater to collect in pools—the earliest oceans.

Chemical clouds
Billowing clouds of steam and chemical gases poured from the Earth. Gravity held most of these near the surface.

Cooling crust over hot interior

Cooler crust
The thin surface crust over the Earth gradually grew thicker. Wherever the crust was cooling and crystallizing, thick clouds of gases bubbled out, building Earth's first atmosphere.

Piercing the skin
As a meteorite landed, hot liquid rock splashed out around the hole in the surface. The meteorite itself plunged into the hot interior. Torrents of lava probably surged up to the hole punched in the surface, spilling out around it in thick sheets.

Large meteorite about to land on the Earth

Flows of lava spreading from the impact crater

Meteorites
These arrivals from space are pieces of an exploded planet, one of the Earth's neighbors that blew up. Some, like this meteorite, are rich in iron and probably came from the core of the exploded planet.

Craters
Meteorites make an impact crater when they land. The impact may be so intense that the meteorite shatters or even evaporates altogether. Meteor Crater in Arizona is 3,936 ft (1,200 m) across and 557 ft (170 m) deep.

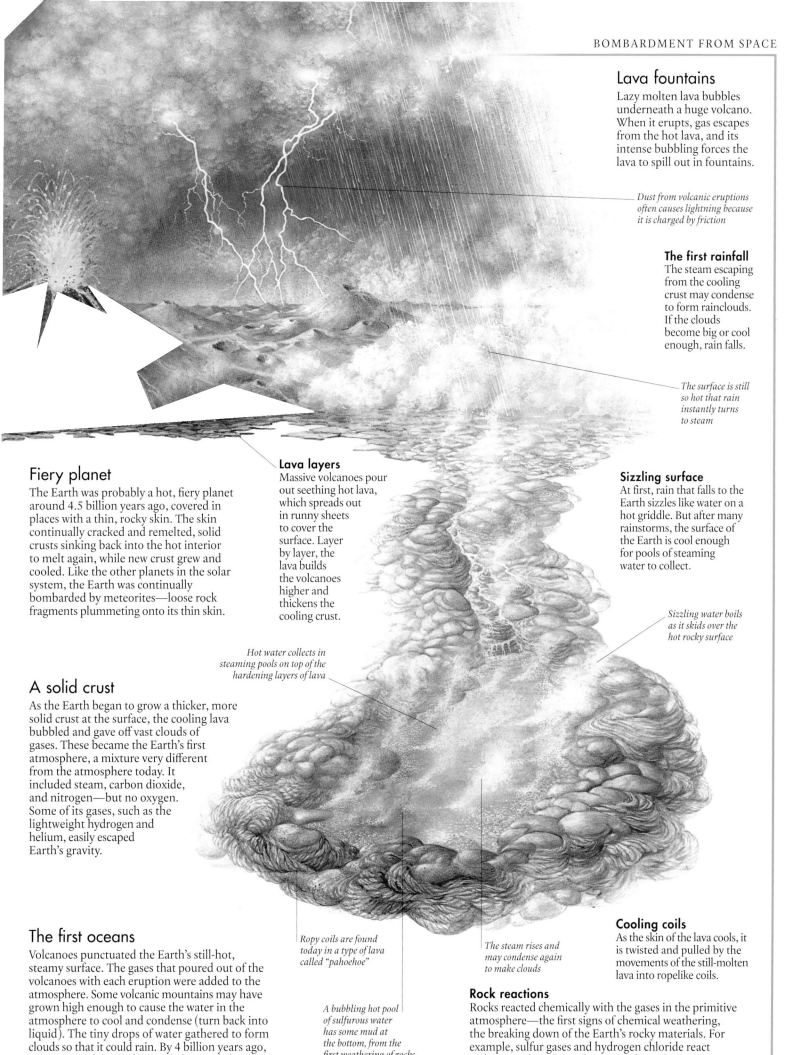

Lava fountains

Lazy molten lava bubbles underneath a huge volcano. When it erupts, gas escapes from the hot lava, and its intense bubbling forces the lava to spill out in fountains.

Dust from volcanic eruptions often causes lightning because it is charged by friction

The first rainfall

The steam escaping from the cooling crust may condense to form rainclouds. If the clouds become big or cool enough, rain falls.

The surface is still so hot that rain instantly turns to steam

Lava layers

Massive volcanoes pour out seething hot lava, which spreads out in runny sheets to cover the surface. Layer by layer, the lava builds the volcanoes higher and thickens the cooling crust.

Sizzling surface

At first, rain that falls to the Earth sizzles like water on a hot griddle. But after many rainstorms, the surface of the Earth is cool enough for pools of steaming water to collect.

Sizzling water boils as it skids over the hot rocky surface

Fiery planet

The Earth was probably a hot, fiery planet around 4.5 billion years ago, covered in places with a thin, rocky skin. The skin continually cracked and remelted, solid crusts sinking back into the hot interior to melt again, while new crust grew and cooled. Like the other planets in the solar system, the Earth was continually bombarded by meteorites—loose rock fragments plummeting onto its thin skin.

A solid crust

As the Earth began to grow a thicker, more solid crust at the surface, the cooling lava bubbled and gave off vast clouds of gases. These became the Earth's first atmosphere, a mixture very different from the atmosphere today. It included steam, carbon dioxide, and nitrogen—but no oxygen. Some of its gases, such as the lightweight hydrogen and helium, easily escaped Earth's gravity.

Hot water collects in steaming pools on top of the hardening layers of lava

The first oceans

Volcanoes punctuated the Earth's still-hot, steamy surface. The gases that poured out of the volcanoes with each eruption were added to the atmosphere. Some volcanic mountains may have grown high enough to cause the water in the atmosphere to cool and condense (turn back into liquid). The tiny drops of water gathered to form clouds so that it could rain. By 4 billion years ago, some parts of the surface cooled enough for rain to collect in the first hot oceans.

Ropy coils are found today in a type of lava called "pahoehoe"

A bubbling hot pool of sulfurous water has some mud at the bottom, from the first weathering of rocks

The steam rises and may condense again to make clouds

Cooling coils

As the skin of the lava cools, it is twisted and pulled by the movements of the still-molten lava into ropelike coils.

Rock reactions

Rocks reacted chemically with the gases in the primitive atmosphere—the first signs of chemical weathering, the breaking down of the Earth's rocky materials. For example, sulfur gases and hydrogen chloride react with minerals in the rocks to transform them into clay minerals, forming the first muds on Earth.

The Age of the Earth

PLANET EARTH IS 4,500 million years old. The first 3,500 million years of Earth history contain the events that still shape its surface: the first solid crust, the first life, the origins of the continents and the atmosphere, and the beginnings of plate tectonics. These events are recorded in the rocks that formed during this time. About 540 million years ago, there was a great explosion of life, and gradually the range of different plants and animals that now populate the Earth came into being. The remains of some of these life forms are captured in the rocks as fossils. These allow geologists to build up a picture of the Earth's long history.

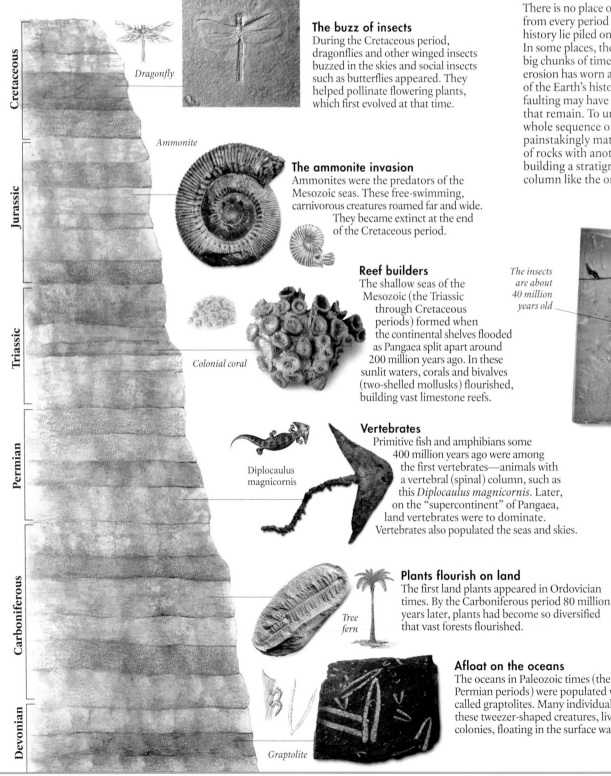

Dragonfly

The buzz of insects
During the Cretaceous period, dragonflies and other winged insects buzzed in the skies and social insects such as butterflies appeared. They helped pollinate flowering plants, which first evolved at that time.

Ammonite

The ammonite invasion
Ammonites were the predators of the Mesozoic seas. These free-swimming, carnivorous creatures roamed far and wide. They became extinct at the end of the Cretaceous period.

Reef builders
The shallow seas of the Mesozoic (the Triassic through Cretaceous periods) formed when the continental shelves flooded as Pangaea split apart around 200 million years ago. In these sunlit waters, corals and bivalves (two-shelled mollusks) flourished, building vast limestone reefs.

Colonial coral

Vertebrates
Primitive fish and amphibians some 400 million years ago were among the first vertebrates—animals with a vertebral (spinal) column, such as this *Diplocaulus magnicornis*. Later, on the "supercontinent" of Pangaea, land vertebrates were to dominate. Vertebrates also populated the seas and skies.

Diplocaulus magnicornis

Plants flourish on land
The first land plants appeared in Ordovician times. By the Carboniferous period 80 million years later, plants had become so diversified that vast forests flourished.

Tree fern

Afloat on the oceans
The oceans in Paleozoic times (the Cambrian through Permian periods) were populated with marine animals called graptolites. Many individual graptolites, such as these tweezer-shaped creatures, lived together in colonies, floating in the surface waters.

Graptolite

History in the layers
There is no place on Earth where rocks from every period throughout geological history lie piled one on top of another. In some places, the rock layers represent big chunks of time, but in most places, erosion has worn away millions of years of the Earth's history, and folding and faulting may have jumbled the layers that remain. To understand the whole sequence of time, geologists painstakingly match up one set of rocks with another, gradually building a stratigraphic (layered) column like the one on the far left.

The insects are about 40 million years old

Trapped in amber
Not all fossils are found in rocks. These gnatlike insects are trapped in amber, a sticky resin that seeps from pine trees. The amber hardened, preserving their bodies.

Cretaceous

Jurassic

Triassic

Permian

Carboniferous

Devonian

How geological time is divided

Earth's history is divided into units of time: the geological clock below shows long eons split into shorter periods. The Hadean, Archean, and Proterozoic eons are known as Precambrian time. The last 540 million years are known as the Phanerozoic eon.

Antarctica's icy cap
Antarctica separated from the other southern continents 35 million years ago. The snow that formed its ice cap began to collect.

First flowers
Flowering plants such as the magnolia appeared in the Cretaceous, at the same time as insects became more diverse.

Humans appear
Human ancestors appeared about 3 million years ago, although modern humans, *Homo sapiens*, did not appear until about 100,000 years ago.

Dinosaurs rule Earth
A great variety of dinosaurs colonized the globe during the Triassic, Jurassic, and Cretaceous periods.

Birth of the Earth
The Earth took shape as one of a family of planets circling around a star, the sun, 4,500 million years ago.

First forests
By Carboniferous times, the land plants had grown into tropical forests.

Mini mammals
The first mammals were small and ratlike.

First fish
The first fish had no jaws.

Solitary satellite
The moon is Earth's only natural satellite. Its oldest rocks are 4,500 million years old. Like the Earth, it was bombarded with meteorites during its first 1,000 million years.

Land plants
The first land plants appeared during Ordovician times.

Oldest rocks on Earth
So far, the oldest rocks found and dated on Earth are 3,800 million years old.

Chordates
Animals with a nerve cord (chordates) were probably ancestors of the vertebrates.

Trilobites
Trilobites scavenged the seabed mud during the Paleozoic era.

Early animals
Fossil sea pens and jellyfish—the first invertebrates—are 700 million years old.

Ancient algae
The oldest fossilized life forms so far found are stromatolites, blue-green algae alive 3,600 million years ago.

Earth history clock

This clock shows what 4,500 million years of Earth history would look like crammed into 12 hours. Precambrian time takes up more than 10 hours. From the explosion of life forms at the beginning of the Cambrian (540 million years ago) to today represents the last 90 minutes. Dinosaurs became extinct just 9 minutes (66 million years) ago. The earliest human ancestors appeared in the very last minute—and the history of *Homo sapiens* (modern humans) occupies just the last second.

Oxygen to ozone
Plants added the first oxygen to the atmosphere. Once there was enough oxygen, a protective ozone layer (above) formed.

Continents
The first continents formed between 3,500 and 2,500 million years ago.

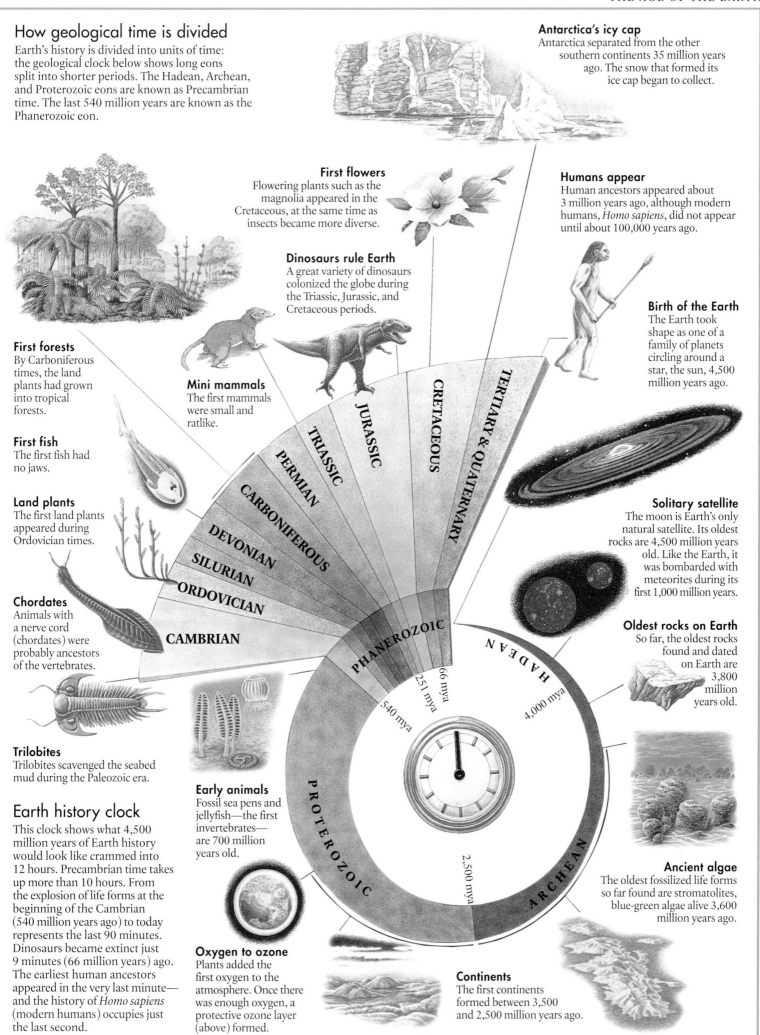

11

Dawn of Earth History

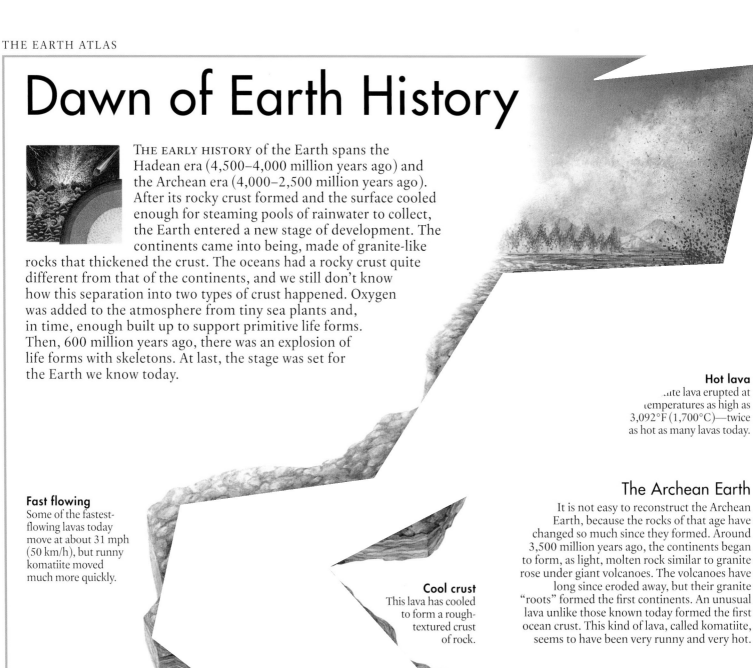

THE EARLY HISTORY of the Earth spans the Hadean era (4,500–4,000 million years ago) and the Archean era (4,000–2,500 million years ago). After its rocky crust formed and the surface cooled enough for steaming pools of rainwater to collect, the Earth entered a new stage of development. The continents came into being, made of granite-like rocks that thickened the crust. The oceans had a rocky crust quite different from that of the continents, and we still don't know how this separation into two types of crust happened. Oxygen was added to the atmosphere from tiny sea plants and, in time, enough built up to support primitive life forms. Then, 600 million years ago, there was an explosion of life forms with skeletons. At last, the stage was set for the Earth we know today.

Hot lava
...ate lava erupted at temperatures as high as 3,092°F (1,700°C)—twice as hot as many lavas today.

The Archean Earth
It is not easy to reconstruct the Archean Earth, because the rocks of that age have changed so much since they formed. Around 3,500 million years ago, the continents began to form, as light, molten rock similar to granite rose under giant volcanoes. The volcanoes have long since eroded away, but their granite "roots" formed the first continents. An unusual lava unlike those known today formed the first ocean crust. This kind of lava, called komatiite, seems to have been very runny and very hot.

Fast flowing
Some of the fastest-flowing lavas today move at about 31 mph (50 km/h), but runny komatiite moved much more quickly.

Cool crust
This lava has cooled to form a rough-textured crust of rock.

Slow the flow
As a lava flow cools, it becomes stickier and more solid, and it slows down.

Traces in the rocks
Today, the only traces of the first ocean floor are tiny rock scraps containing komatiite. It seems that whatever mechanism made this strange lava stopped happening 2,500 million years ago. The modern ocean crust is made from a quite different hardened lava known as basalt.

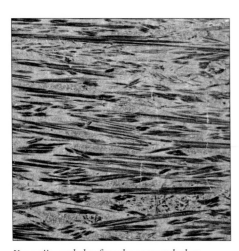

Komatiite cooled to form huge crystals that looked like coarse blades of grass.

A river of lava
When komatiite lava erupts, it melts the rocks that it flows over. As a result, it cuts its path or channel lower and lower, just like a river.

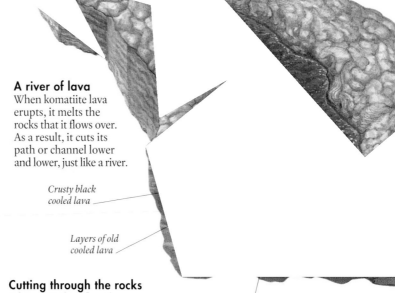

Crusty black cooled lava

Layers of old cooled lava

Cutting through the rocks
A komatiite lava flow that flowed for a week could cut a channel 65 ft (20 m) deep by melting the rocks underneath.

Quick-moving lava shooting through the crusty channel

Long-distance lava
The lava is able to flow through its eroded channel for long distances.

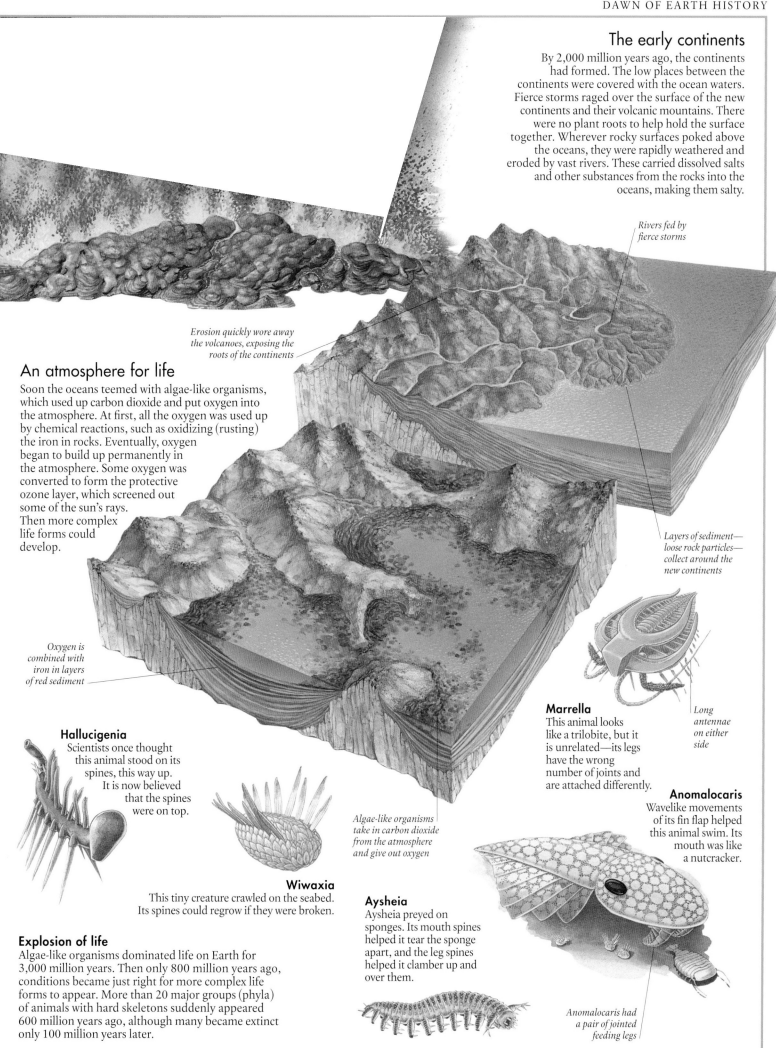

The early continents

By 2,000 million years ago, the continents had formed. The low places between the continents were covered with the ocean waters. Fierce storms raged over the surface of the new continents and their volcanic mountains. There were no plant roots to help hold the surface together. Wherever rocky surfaces poked above the oceans, they were rapidly weathered and eroded by vast rivers. These carried dissolved salts and other substances from the rocks into the oceans, making them salty.

Rivers fed by fierce storms

Erosion quickly wore away the volcanoes, exposing the roots of the continents

An atmosphere for life

Soon the oceans teemed with algae-like organisms, which used up carbon dioxide and put oxygen into the atmosphere. At first, all the oxygen was used up by chemical reactions, such as oxidizing (rusting) the iron in rocks. Eventually, oxygen began to build up permanently in the atmosphere. Some oxygen was converted to form the protective ozone layer, which screened out some of the sun's rays. Then more complex life forms could develop.

Layers of sediment— loose rock particles— collect around the new continents

Oxygen is combined with iron in layers of red sediment

Marrella
This animal looks like a trilobite, but it is unrelated—its legs have the wrong number of joints and are attached differently.

Long antennae on either side

Hallucigenia
Scientists once thought this animal stood on its spines, this way up. It is now believed that the spines were on top.

Algae-like organisms take in carbon dioxide from the atmosphere and give out oxygen

Anomalocaris
Wavelike movements of its fin flap helped this animal swim. Its mouth was like a nutcracker.

Wiwaxia
This tiny creature crawled on the seabed. Its spines could regrow if they were broken.

Aysheia
Aysheia preyed on sponges. Its mouth spines helped it tear the sponge apart, and the leg spines helped it clamber up and over them.

Explosion of life

Algae-like organisms dominated life on Earth for 3,000 million years. Then only 800 million years ago, conditions became just right for more complex life forms to appear. More than 20 major groups (phyla) of animals with hard skeletons suddenly appeared 600 million years ago, although many became extinct only 100 million years later.

Anomalocaris had a pair of jointed feeding legs

The Moving Crust

NOT ONLY IS OUR PLANET spinning through space, but also the Earth's surface is heaving about, though very slowly. Each year, the continents move 1–3 in (2–8 cm) or so—some getting closer together, others moving apart. This sounds like a small amount, but over a million years, it adds up to 12.5–50 miles (20–80 km). The movement happens because the inside of the planet is hot and turbulent. Its motion disturbs the cool rocky surface and makes the huge plates of the crust move around. New ocean floor is made at spreading ridges, only to move over tens or hundreds of millions of years toward a subduction zone, where it is destroyed. This slow movement of the Earth's plates has been going on for thousands of millions of years.

Plate boundaries

A plate edge meets another at three possible kinds of margin. If a plate carrying an ocean meets a continental plate, the ocean crust plunges down, or subducts, under the continent and disappears. When solid rocky crust of one plate crunches sideways against another equally solid plate, the rocks fracture and earthquakes happen. Where two plates move apart, there is a widening crack in the Earth's outer skin, which fills with hot magma rising from the mantle.

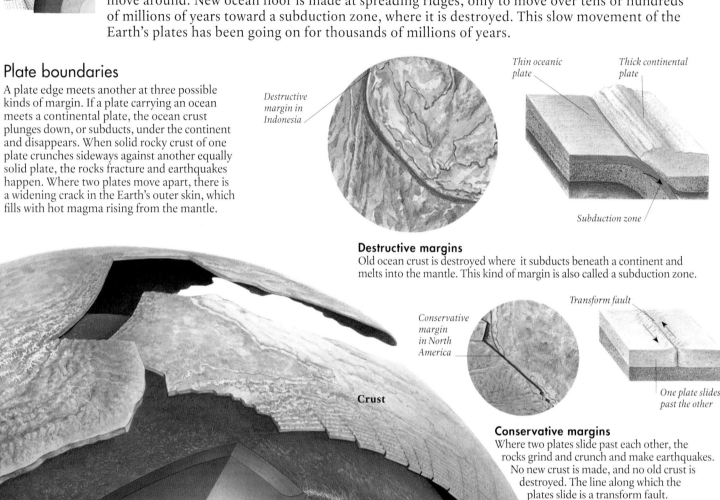

Destructive margin in Indonesia

Thin oceanic plate

Thick continental plate

Subduction zone

Destructive margins
Old ocean crust is destroyed where it subducts beneath a continent and melts into the mantle. This kind of margin is also called a subduction zone.

Conservative margin in North America

Transform fault

One plate slides past the other

Conservative margins
Where two plates slide past each other, the rocks grind and crunch and make earthquakes. No new crust is made, and no old crust is destroyed. The line along which the plates slide is a transform fault.

Constructive margin in the Atlantic Ocean

Magma oozing up from the mantle

Crust

Topmost mantle (lithosphere)

Mantle (asthenosphere)

Core

Lower and transitional mantle

Earth's turbulent mantle
The mantle is more or less solid, but over long periods of time—millions, or tens of millions of years—it flows like a thick, sticky plastic. Some parts of the mantle are cooler and more solid than others. Other regions, under constructive margins and volcanoes, are hotter and contain some liquid, which will rise to become magma.

Constructive margins
New ocean crust is made where plates are spreading apart. The gap between the plates fills with magma. These margins are also known as spreading ridges.

Drifting continents

Continual shifting and drifting of the plates that cover the Earth's surface is what changes the shapes of the continents and oceans. Three stages in one continent's drift toward another are shown here. Old ocean crust is swallowed and destroyed at a subduction zone. At the same time, a new ocean grows at the far margin of the plate. Eventually, the entire ocean crust disappears back into the mantle, bringing the two continents together. Continental crust cannot subduct; it is too light in weight to go down into the mantle. Instead, it grafts onto the other continent.

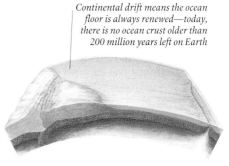

Ocean crust meets this continent and subducts

Plates pushed apart to make room for the new crust

Topmost mantle

Ocean crust

Spreading ridge

Continental crust

Subduction zone

The ocean floor spreads as magma rises to plug the gap between plates, only to be added to the plate edges

Continental drift means the ocean floor is always renewed—today, there is no ocean crust older than 200 million years left on Earth

First push
A spreading ridge pushes one continent toward another. The ocean between them has nowhere to go and begins to subduct at the edge of the faraway continent.

The push continues
As the new ocean grows bigger, the old ocean gets smaller. Some of the old ocean crust is melted at the subduction zone. It rises to feed volcanoes at the surface, and a mountain range starts to grow.

The continents meet
The mountains buckle up and fold as the continents come closer. Finally, there is no more old ocean crust left to subduct. The continents meet, and one grafts onto another, making a bigger continent.

The world long ago

The shapes and locations of the continents and oceans were very different in times gone by. It is easy to put together the history of the last two hundred million years, by imagining that today's ocean crust is no longer there. In this way, we know that two hundred million years ago there was a giant continent, called Pangaea. This supercontinent came about through the collision and grafting together of even older continents. It is not so easy to reconstruct what happened before Pangaea. There was an even earlier supercontinent, also pieced together from even older continents, which themselves had been formed by previous continental splitting.

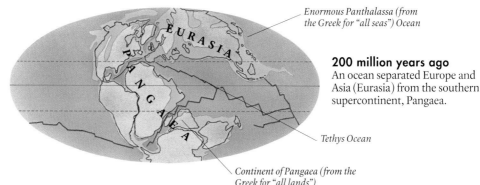

Enormous Panthalassa (from the Greek for "all seas") Ocean

Tethys Ocean

Continent of Pangaea (from the Greek for "all lands")

200 million years ago
An ocean separated Europe and Asia (Eurasia) from the southern supercontinent, Pangaea.

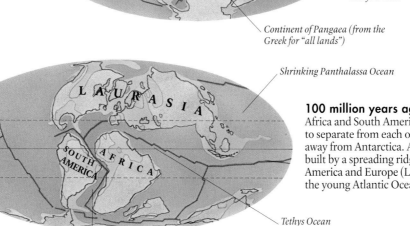

Shrinking Panthalassa Ocean

Tethys Ocean

Atlantic Ocean

100 million years ago
Africa and South America had already begun to separate from each other as they broke away from Antarctica. As new ocean floor was built by a spreading ridge between North America and Europe (Laurasia) and Africa, the young Atlantic Ocean was born.

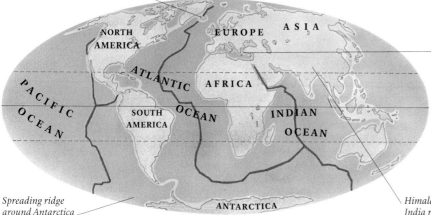

Iceland is made of oceanic crust

Remains of Tethys Ocean

Present day
Antarctica is now separated from all the other continents; it is totally surrounded by new ocean floor, which has been made by a spreading ridge encircling it.

Spreading ridge around Antarctica

Himalayas formed where India rammed into Asia

Lines of Fire

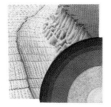

Most volcanoes lie along lines of fire that encircle the planet. These lines are plate boundaries. Many earthquakes also happen near these cracks. This uneven distribution on the Earth was noticed early in the 19th century, though at that time there was no way of explaining why it should be. An especially large number of volcanoes and earthquakes happen around the shores of the Pacific Ocean, shown here. This explosive area is sometimes called the Pacific Ring of Fire. Its amazing landscapes are a result of its fiery nature.

The Valley of Ten Thousand Smokes
A huge ashy eruption blanketed this valley in Alaska, in 1912. The first explorers to venture into the valley saw countless bubbling volcanic "smokes" rising from the ash. The ash itself is up to 164 ft (50 m) deep in places.

Key to map
Three types of boundaries between plates are shown on this map: constructive margins are red, destructive margins are brown, and conservative margins are purple. See the previous pages for an explanation of these terms.

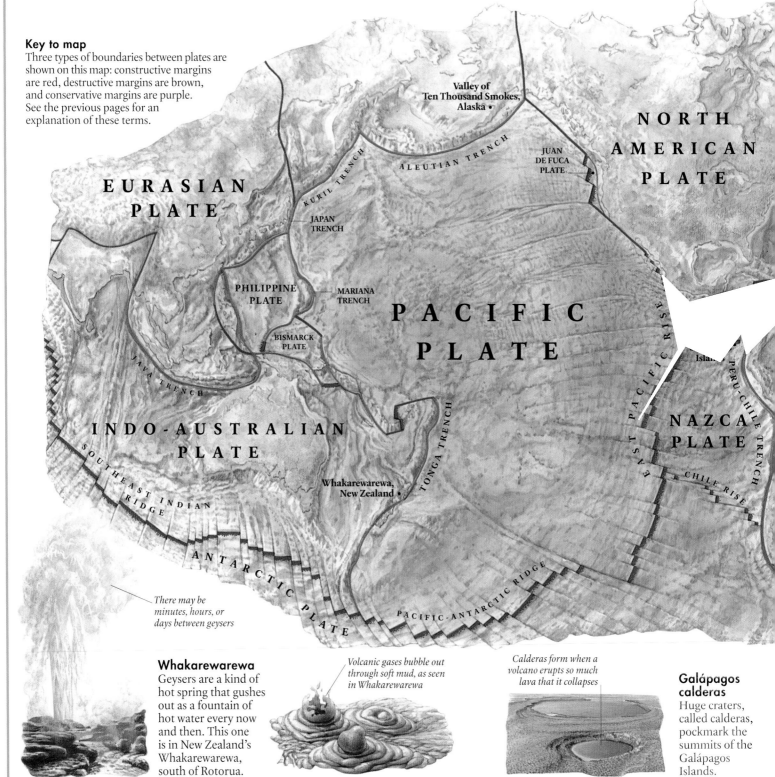

Valley of Ten Thousand Smokes, Alaska •

NORTH AMERICAN PLATE

JUAN DE FUCA PLATE

ALEUTIAN TRENCH

EURASIAN PLATE

KURIL TRENCH

JAPAN TRENCH

PHILIPPINE PLATE

MARIANA TRENCH

BISMARCK PLATE

PACIFIC PLATE

JAVA TRENCH

Islan...

EAST PACIFIC RISE

PERU-CHILE TRENCH

NAZCA PLATE

CHILE RISE

INDO-AUSTRALIAN PLATE

SOUTHEAST INDIAN RIDGE

TONGA TRENCH

Whakarewarewa, New Zealand •

ANTARCTIC PLATE

PACIFIC-ANTARCTIC RIDGE

There may be minutes, hours, or days between geysers

Whakarewarewa
Geysers are a kind of hot spring that gushes out as a fountain of hot water every now and then. This one is in New Zealand's Whakarewarewa, south of Rotorua.

Volcanic gases bubble out through soft mud, as seen in Whakarewarewa

Calderas form when a volcano erupts so much lava that it collapses

Galápagos calderas
Huge craters, called calderas, pockmark the summits of the Galápagos Islands.

Surtsey born from the sea

In 1963, a bubbling volcano broke through the waves south of Iceland. The new island, named Surtsey after an ancient Icelandic fire god, grew larger as more and more lava poured out over the first loose ash layers. Surtsey is now home to a variety of plants, insects, and birds.

Surtsey sits astride the Mid-Atlantic Ridge, where two of the Earth's plates are slowly pulling apart. New magma from inside the Earth cools to heal the crack, making new ocean crust.

A lot of activity

About 30 volcanoes are erupting in any one year. Of these, some continue to erupt for several years, or even decades, while others may erupt only once during that time. One or two have been active for thousands of years. Thousands of earthquakes happen each year, but most are far too small to be noticed. A few dozen cause shaking that can be felt, and fewer than 10 are really large.

Fingal's Cave

The basalt columns that built the island of Staffa off western Scotland are formed from lava that cracked into regular shapes as it cooled slowly, 60 million years ago.

REYKJANES RIDGE

EURASIAN PLATE

- Surtsey, Iceland
- Fingal's Cave, Scotland
- Le Puy, France

ANATOLIAN PLATE

IRANIAN PLATE

ARABIAN PLATE

Karum Pillars, Ethiopia •

AFRICAN PLATE

SOUTH AMERICAN PLATE

MID-ATLANTIC RIDGE

Réunion •

ATLANTIC-INDIAN RIDGE

SCOTIA PLATE

ANTARCTIC PLATE

Le Puy, France

This church in southern France is built atop a volcanic rock 250 ft (76 m) high. The rock hardened inside the volcano two million years ago. It was exposed when softer, ashy rocks were eroded away from around it.

Karum salt pillars

Rain weathers salt out from volcanic rocks, washing it into the Assale Lake in Ethiopia. The water is so salty that the surface crystallizes over, with salt pillars growing 10 ft (3 m) overnight.

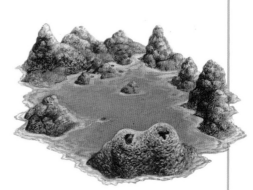

Signs of the times

Old, eroded volcanic features in the landscape are an indication that millions, or even tens of millions of years ago, there were volcanoes there. Not all of these features lie along the lines of fire we know today. This means the old lines were in different places and shows that the Earth's plates move as time passes. This movement is evidence of change in the churning motions of the Earth's turbulent interior.

Réunion

One of the Earth's largest volcanoes is Réunion island, which rises from the deep ocean floor to its summit craters, 10,068 ft (3,069 m) above sea level.

Explosive Volcanoes

ON MAY 18, 1980, the entire volcano of Mount St. Helens (shown here) exploded. Explosive volcanoes like this produce thick, sticky lava, and erupt infrequently. Between eruptions, there is time for gas to build up in the magma below the volcano. Eventually, the pressure of the gas blows the overlying rocks apart. The gassy lava froths up and explodes, shattering into tiny fragments. Propelled by the force of the explosion and the continuing release of gas, the fragmented lava billows out. It launches down the steep slope of the volcano as a high-speed ash flow, engulfing everything in its path.

Fire mountain

Mount St. Helens is shown on the right, with two sections pulled away to expose its explosive center. The last major eruption had been in the 1800s, so the volcano had been silent for over a hundred years before its devastating eruption in 1980. Mount St. Helens at last lived up to the name given to it by its native peoples—Tahonelatchah, or "fire mountain."

Eruption cloud

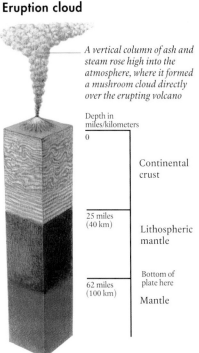

A vertical column of ash and steam rose high into the atmosphere, where it formed a mushroom cloud directly over the erupting volcano

Depth in miles/kilometers

0

Continental crust

25 miles (40 km)

Lithospheric mantle

62 miles (100 km)

Bottom of plate here

Mantle

Magma

Magma is generated about 62 miles (100 km) under the ground. It rises through the solid rock in blobs, and collects in a reservoir. During decades or even centuries of slow cooling, the magma crystallizes and gas bubbles rise to the top. When pressure is suddenly released in an eruption, pressure from the gas blows out the crystals and explodes the magma, which chills to lava or glass and falls as ash.

A cloud of ash
The dense cloud of ash from a large eruption may rise 19 miles (30 km) or more into the atmosphere. Winds can carry the choking cloud over great distances. Ash from Mount St. Helens spread more than 150 miles (240 km) in just two hours.

Hot ash
The temperature inside the cloud reached 680°F (315°C).

The eruption blew out the side of the mountain

Mud flows
Glaciers on the volcano slopes were suddenly melted in the eruption, causing destructive mud flows.

Section of mountainside removed to show the interior of the volcano

Below the volcano
Lava crystallizes slowly in the magma reservoir below the volcano. The arrival of a new blob of magma from greater depth below may trigger an eruption.

Bubbling under
As the magma rises, the gases contained in it escape and form larger and larger bubbles. These balloon out against the rock, trying to find an escape route.

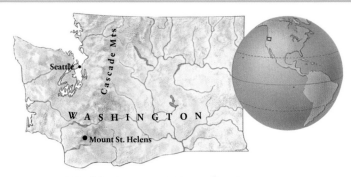

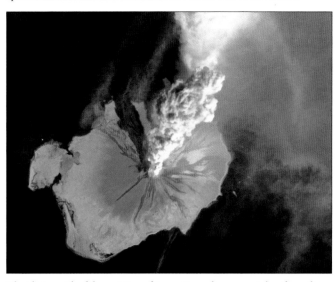

Bird's eye view

This color-enhanced photograph of Augustine volcano in Alaska, shows the explosive force of an ashy eruption. The plume of ash rises high into the atmosphere, then rains down. Traces of ash clouds can spread right around the Earth, affecting the weather and creating spectacular sunrises and sunsets on the other side of the world.

The photograph of the eruption of Augustine volcano was taken from the safety of a Landsat satellite. The ash cloud is about 7 miles (11 km) high.

Washington state's Cascades Range

Mount St. Helens is a volcano in the Cascades mountain range, along the northwestern coast of North America.

Avalanche

After a small earthquake shook the volcano, its entire north face trembled slightly then suddenly broke loose to slide downhill as a massive avalanche.

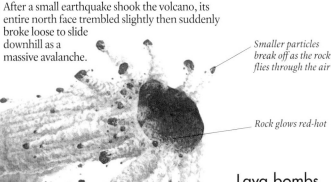

Smaller particles break off as the rock flies through the air

Rock glows red-hot

Lava bombs

Blocks of hot rock and new magma were catapulted out of the explosion cloud, traveling even faster than the ash cloud itself. Fragments of new lava are known as pyroclasts, meaning fiery fragments. Many are tiny, but together they make up devastating ash flows, which sear every living thing they meet. Ash flows and the clouds flash with lightning bolts and may cause torrential rain storms.

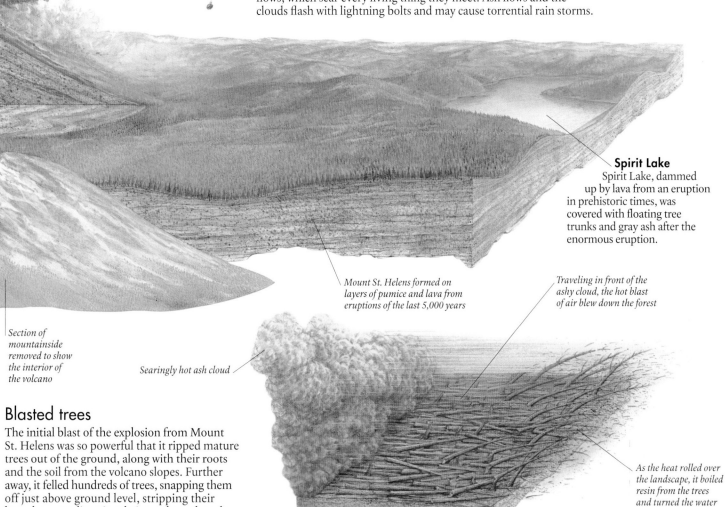

Section of mountainside removed to show the interior of the volcano

Spirit Lake

Spirit Lake, dammed up by lava from an eruption in prehistoric times, was covered with floating tree trunks and gray ash after the enormous eruption.

Mount St. Helens formed on layers of pumice and lava from eruptions of the last 5,000 years

Traveling in front of the ashy cloud, the hot blast of air blew down the forest

Searingly hot ash cloud

Blasted trees

The initial blast of the explosion from Mount St. Helens was so powerful that it ripped mature trees out of the ground, along with their roots and the soil from the volcano slopes. Further away, it felled hundreds of trees, snapping them off just above ground level, stripping their branches, or splintering their trunks as though they were flimsy matchwood.

As the heat rolled over the landscape, it boiled resin from the trees and turned the water in plants and animals instantly into steam

Lava Eruptions

IN A VIOLENT ERUPTION, an explosive volcano can devastate the land and throw clouds of searing hot ash into the sky. But other types of volcanoes erupt more quietly and gently, oozing floods of runny, red-hot magma from deep within the Earth's mantle. Because this erupted lava cools to a dark-colored rock called basalt, these volcanoes are known as basalt lava volcanoes. Basalt lava volcanoes usually erupt quite frequently, so they do not build up a huge head of pressure. Instead, the volcano may spit fountains of lava into the air, along with long lava flows that spread out over the surrounding countryside. Over time, these eruptions build huge, broad mountains with very gentle slopes. The islands of Iceland and Hawaii were formed in this way.

This volcano has not erupted for about four million years. The oldest islands are growing smaller as they slowly sink into the sea.

Sediment worn from the islands buries their bases

Islands of fire

The island of Hawaii lies in the middle of a great plate underlying much of the Pacific Ocean. Two of the largest and most active volcanoes on Earth—Mauna Loa and Kilauea—are found here. In this illustration, Mauna Loa is split in half to reveal its red-hot interior. Basalt magma from a hot spot in the mantle wells up beneath the volcano, sometimes erupting near its summit. If the magma finds a crack inside the volcano and spreads out sideways, lava may come out from lower on the volcano slopes.

PACIFIC OCEAN

KAUAI
NIIHAU
OAHU
MOLOKAI
LANAI
MAUI
KAHOOLAWE
HAWAII

Hawaiian island chain

The Hawaiian Islands are the tops of huge volcanoes rising from the Pacific Ocean floor. Hawaii is the largest and youngest of a chain of 130 islands. The eight largest islands are seen above.

The volcanoes grow older the further they have been carried from the hot spot.

Older volcanoes are no longer active.

Hot spot volcanoes

The formation of the Hawaiian Islands was a puzzle to geologists, because unlike most volcanoes, they are in the middle of a plate. By determining the age of the volcanoes, geologists reasoned that the entire chain had formed over a stationary "hot spot" deep in the mantle. A volcano forms over the hot spot, but as the plate carrying it moves, the volcano stops erupting and a new, younger volcano forms. In this way, the hot spot builds a chain of volcanoes that increase in age the further away they are found from the hot spot.

The youngest volcano forms right over the hot spot, and erupts frequently.

The plate is now moving northwestward along this path at about 4 in (10 cm) a year.

Each volcano stays over the hot spot for about a million years.

Hot spots in the mantle appear to stay fixed in position for tens of millions of years. Some hot spots are found under continents.

Hidden depths

Measured from the ocean bed, Mauna Loa is over 29,500 ft (9,000 m) tall—one of the largest volcanoes on Earth.

Pillows on the seabed

When hot lava erupts under cold water, pillow lavas form. These are rounded blobs of lava with a thin skin. Inside the skin, red hot lava continues to flow until eventually the skin splits and another pillow-shaped blob begins to form. This happens again and again until a jumble of pillows piles up on the seabed.

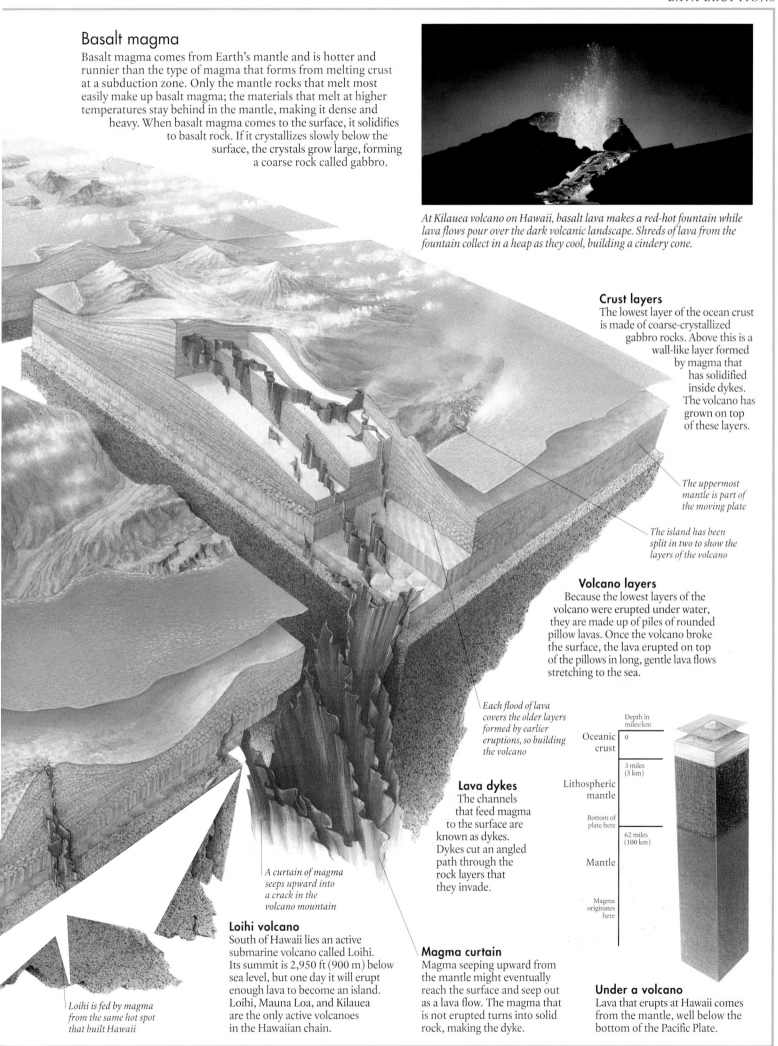

Basalt magma

Basalt magma comes from Earth's mantle and is hotter and runnier than the type of magma that forms from melting crust at a subduction zone. Only the mantle rocks that melt most easily make up basalt magma; the materials that melt at higher temperatures stay behind in the mantle, making it dense and heavy. When basalt magma comes to the surface, it solidifies to basalt rock. If it crystallizes slowly below the surface, the crystals grow large, forming a coarse rock called gabbro.

At Kilauea volcano on Hawaii, basalt lava makes a red-hot fountain while lava flows pour over the dark volcanic landscape. Shreds of lava from the fountain collect in a heap as they cool, building a cindery cone.

Crust layers

The lowest layer of the ocean crust is made of coarse-crystallized gabbro rocks. Above this is a wall-like layer formed by magma that has solidified inside dykes. The volcano has grown on top of these layers.

The uppermost mantle is part of the moving plate

The island has been split in two to show the layers of the volcano

Volcano layers

Because the lowest layers of the volcano were erupted under water, they are made up of piles of rounded pillow lavas. Once the volcano broke the surface, the lava erupted on top of the pillows in long, gentle lava flows stretching to the sea.

Each flood of lava covers the older layers formed by earlier eruptions, so building the volcano

Lava dykes

The channels that feed magma to the surface are known as dykes. Dykes cut an angled path through the rock layers that they invade.

A curtain of magma seeps upward into a crack in the volcano mountain

Loihi volcano

South of Hawaii lies an active submarine volcano called Loihi. Its summit is 2,950 ft (900 m) below sea level, but one day it will erupt enough lava to become an island. Loihi, Mauna Loa, and Kilauea are the only active volcanoes in the Hawaiian chain.

Loihi is fed by magma from the same hot spot that built Hawaii

Magma curtain

Magma seeping upward from the mantle might eventually reach the surface and seep out as a lava flow. The magma that is not erupted turns into solid rock, making the dyke.

Depth in miles/km	
Oceanic crust	0
Lithospheric mantle	3 miles (5 km)
	Bottom of plate here
Mantle	62 miles (100 km)
	Magma originates here

Under a volcano

Lava that erupts at Hawaii comes from the mantle, well below the bottom of the Pacific Plate.

Shaking the Crust

WHEN ROCK MASSES under stress suddenly slip apart and break, the crust trembles in an earthquake. Stress can build up for years in the rock before it is swiftly released. The broken rock moves along a crack called a fault. Most are underground, but some faults break through to the surface and may even show up in the landscape. The Alpine Fault in New Zealand, shown on these pages, has divided the landscape in two, with rising mountains on the east side and plain lands to the west of the fault line.

New Zealand
The junction of two plates runs right through the North and South islands of New Zealand, in the Pacific Ocean.

NORTH ISLAND

SOUTH ISLAND

Southern Alps

Why earthquakes happen
The three steps below show how stress building in the rocks along a fault line may lead to an earthquake. Two sliding plates lock together, and pressure builds along the fault line. The stress builds up until the strength of the rocks is overcome. The plates suddenly unlock and move, causing an earthquake. The main illustration shows a quake along New Zealand's Alpine Fault.

Stress builds
One plate is moving past another, but the fault line where they meet has got stuck. Stress builds up in the rocks at each side of the fault.

Stress against strength
The stress deforms the rocks, and cracks open in them. Eventually the stress is greater than the strength of the rocks.

Earthquake
When their strength is overcome, the rocks break and an earthquake happens.

Volcanic landscapes— from geysers to active volcanoes—are found on North Island

Breaking point
The place where the rock starts to break is called the focus of the earthquake, and the point above, on the Earth's surface, is the epicenter.

The earthquake's vibrations travel out from its focus in all directions

SOUTH

Alpine Fault

SOUTHERN ALPS

Mt. Tasman

Mt. Cook

Mt. Sefton

Focus ... quake

Up and down
The New Zealand Alps grow a little higher with each quake, but they are eroded as fast as they are pushed up.

Section of main artwork pulled out and made larger

River courses moved apart along the fault line

Rocks near the surface at the fault are crushed to a greenish rocky mush, which erodes easily

Deeper down, rocks in the fault plane may be melted by heat caused by friction

Fault plane
The fault plane is unlikely to be a straight line; it is probably wavy. The irregularities are part of what makes the fault stick between quakes. The more firmly it sticks, the longer time it will be until the next quake and the bigger that quake will be.

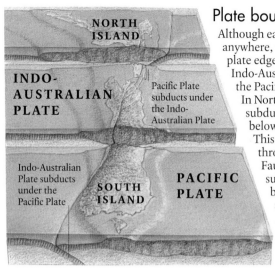

Plate boundaries

Although earthquakes can strike anywhere, they are most common near plate edges. South of New Zealand, the Indo-Australian Plate is diving beneath the Pacific Plate in a subduction zone. In North Island, the Pacific Plate is subducting in the other direction, below the Indo-Australian Plate. This results in a gigantic tear through South Island—the Alpine Fault. In North Island, the subduction causes earthquakes, both in the diving Pacific Plate and the overriding Indo-Australian Plate.

NORTH ISLAND

INDO-AUSTRALIAN PLATE

Pacific Plate subducts under the Indo-Australian Plate

Indo-Australian Plate subducts under the Pacific Plate

SOUTH ISLAND

PACIFIC PLATE

San Francisco, California, sits astride the San Andreas Fault. This photo shows a road split apart during a huge earthquake in 1906.

Earthquake waves

The vibrations that travel out from the focus are called seismic waves. These move fastest through dense rocks and more slowly through loose sediments and water. Different kinds of waves cause the rocks to vibrate in different ways. The two kinds that travel fastest are P-waves (primary) and S-waves (secondary). After the vibrations pass, there is no sign of change to hard, solid rocks, but soft sediments may be compacted and pressed together.

Primary waves
P-waves compress and stretch rocks they pass through. Their simple push-and-pull movement lets the waves travel fast.

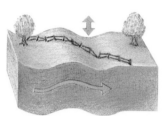

Secondary waves
S-waves move up and down, and also sideways in all directions at the same time.

Shaken to the foundations
Shaking ground can collapse buildings, bridges, and other structures. The damage is often most intense nearest to the epicenter.

Sometimes the most damaging vibrations are intensified by soft rocks, where the vibrations travel more slowly

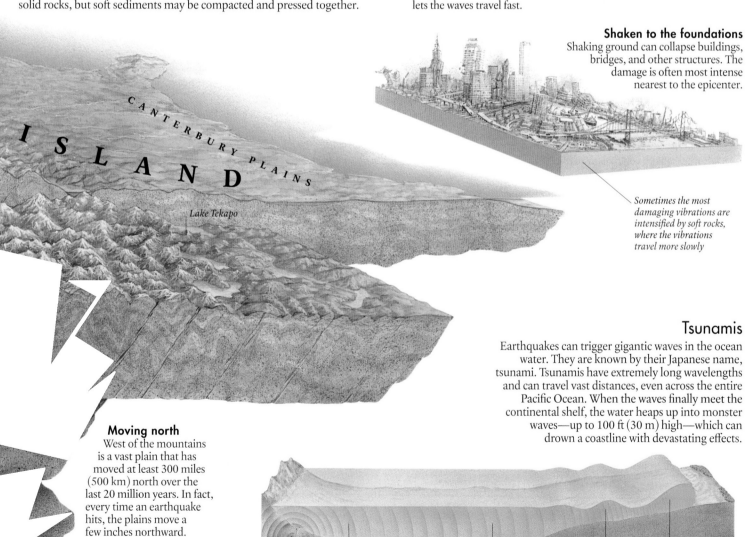

CANTERBURY PLAINS

ISLAND

Lake Tekapo

Tsunamis

Earthquakes can trigger gigantic waves in the ocean water. They are known by their Japanese name, tsunami. Tsunamis have extremely long wavelengths and can travel vast distances, even across the entire Pacific Ocean. When the waves finally meet the continental shelf, the water heaps up into monster waves—up to 100 ft (30 m) high—which can drown a coastline with devastating effects.

Moving north
West of the mountains is a vast plain that has moved at least 300 miles (500 km) north over the last 20 million years. In fact, every time an earthquake hits, the plains move a few inches northward.

An underwater earthquake causes seabed rocks to break along the fault plane

The displaced rocks disturb the water above, generating waves

The train of waves travels through the water away from the epicenter

At the continental shelf, the water heaps up into huge waves

A very high surging flood hits the shore about every 10 minutes

23

Mountain Building

As SOON AS mountains are lifted up, erosion starts to wear them away. The higher the mountains become, the more rain and snow fall on them—and the more the mountains are carved down by water and ice. Tall, rugged mountains are an indication that mountain building is still taking place. Once there is no more uplift, erosion takes over, and the mountains are worn lower, until eventually only hills remain. Even these contain clues within their rocks to their past as a lofty mountain range.

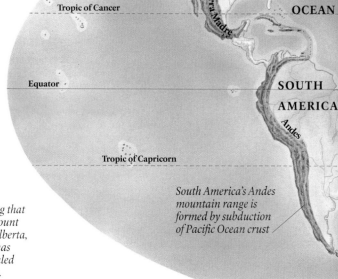

The Rocky Mountains grew as subducting ocean crust carried islands to the edge of the coast and packed them together to add to the mountains

South America's Andes mountain range is formed by subduction of Pacific Ocean crust

The folding that formed Mount Head in Alberta, Canada, has been revealed by erosion.

Kilimanjaro, Tanzania
An old volcano built of alternating layers of ash and lava, Kilimanjaro is the highest point in Africa at 19,344 ft (5,896 m).

Elbrus, Russian Federation
Elbrus is 18,510 ft (5,642 m) high. It is a volcano, but it has not been active for many thousands of years.

Mt. McKinley, US
Mt. McKinley stands glacier-clad 20,322 ft (6,194 m) high in the Denali National Park in Alaska.

Snow line
The snow line falls lower the farther the mountain is from the equator.

Kilimanjaro is on the equator, but it has a permanent ice cap.

Because Elbrus is farther from the equator, the snow line is lower.

At Mt. McKinley, the tree line drops with the snow line.

In the polar regions, permanent ice exists at sea level.

Tree line
Lower than the snow line is the tree line; above it, trees find it impossible to grow because of the cold.

Snowy tops
Near the equator, where the direct angle of the sun's rays warms the land, the snow line is over 19,686 ft (6,000 m) up. Only at such heights is it cool enough for permanent ice to exist. Away from the equator, where the sun's heat rays heat the land less, the snow line is progressively lower. Sections of three mountains, at different distances from the equator, are shown here.

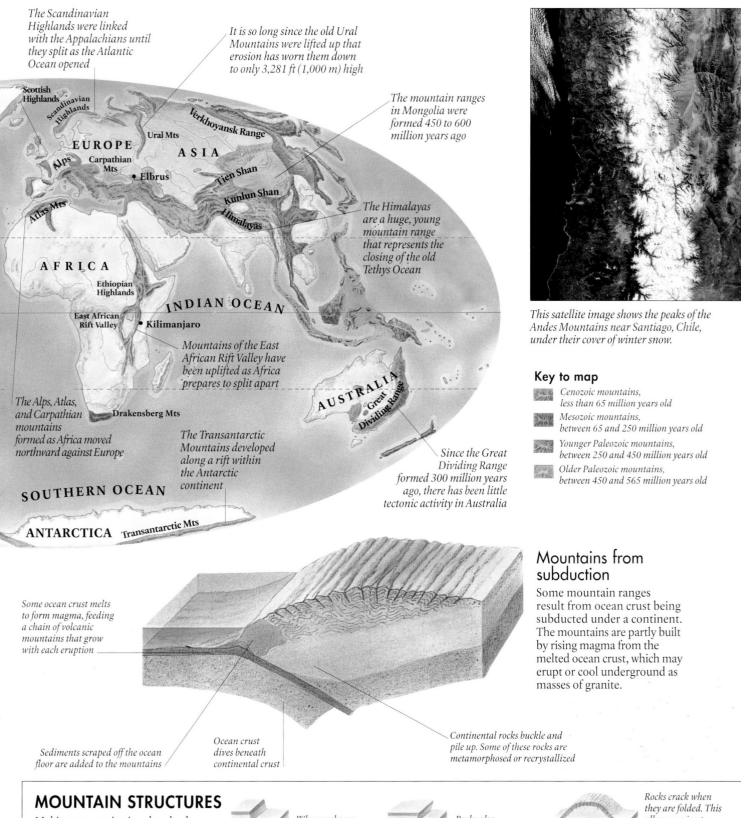

The Scandinavian Highlands were linked with the Appalachians until they split as the Atlantic Ocean opened

It is so long since the old Ural Mountains were lifted up that erosion has worn them down to only 3,281 ft (1,000 m) high

The mountain ranges in Mongolia were formed 450 to 600 million years ago

Scottish Highlands

Scandinavian Highlands

EUROPE

Ural Mts

Verkhoyansk Range

ASIA

Alps

Carpathian Mts

• Elbrus

Tien Shan

Kunlun Shan

Himalayas

Atlas Mts

The Himalayas are a huge, young mountain range that represents the closing of the old Tethys Ocean

AFRICA

Ethiopian Highlands

INDIAN OCEAN

East African Rift Valley

• Kilimanjaro

Mountains of the East African Rift Valley have been uplifted as Africa prepares to split apart

AUSTRALIA

Great Dividing Range

The Alps, Atlas, and Carpathian mountains formed as Africa moved northward against Europe

The Transantarctic Mountains developed along a rift within the Antarctic continent

Drakensberg Mts

Since the Great Dividing Range formed 300 million years ago, there has been little tectonic activity in Australia

SOUTHERN OCEAN

ANTARCTICA   Transantarctic Mts

This satellite image shows the peaks of the Andes Mountains near Santiago, Chile, under their cover of winter snow.

Key to map

Cenozoic mountains, less than 65 million years old

Mesozoic mountains, between 65 and 250 million years old

Younger Paleozoic mountains, between 250 and 450 million years old

Older Paleozoic mountains, between 450 and 565 million years old

Mountains from subduction

Some mountain ranges result from ocean crust being subducted under a continent. The mountains are partly built by rising magma from the melted ocean crust, which may erupt or cool underground as masses of granite.

Some ocean crust melts to form magma, feeding a chain of volcanic mountains that grow with each eruption

Sediments scraped off the ocean floor are added to the mountains

Ocean crust dives beneath continental crust

Continental rocks buckle and pile up. Some of these rocks are metamorphosed or recrystallized

MOUNTAIN STRUCTURES

Making mountains involves both stretching and compression. These illustrations show different types of folding and fracturing, which may be seen in mountain ranges.

When rocks are stretched apart, they fracture. This is a normal fault.

Rocks also fracture when they are compressed. This is a reverse fault.

Rocks crack when they are folded. This allows erosion to wear them away faster. So the tops of upfolds do not become the tops of mountains.

Folded rocks
The layered sediments begin to fold as the rocks of the crust become more and more compressed.

Faulted fold
When the folding is so intense the rocks cannot bend any more, they break, forming a thrust fault.

Folds and faults
In a mountain range, layers of rock are squeezed and folded, then may fracture to form thrust faults. Erosion wears away the tops of the thrust mass of rocks to make the mountain peaks.

Continents Collide

OVER THE LAST 70 MILLION YEARS, a mighty collision between two continents has created the Himalayan mountain range. The continent of India began to move slowly northward toward Asia, swallowing up an old ocean in its path. Some small continents in the ocean were pushed into Asia first, forming the young Himalayas. As the two continents came closer together, the ocean floor was subducted. When all the ocean had been subducted, India finally met up with the Asian mountains. India has continued to move northward, and Asia has buckled and been pushed up, forming the world's highest mountains and highest plateau.

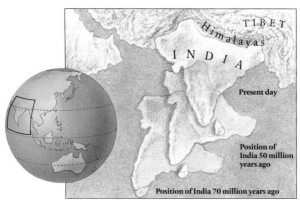

India's northward charge

Before its collision with Asia, the plate carrying India was moving north at 4 in (10 cm) a year. Once the continents met, this slowed to 2 in (5 cm) a year. The Himalayas are the youngest mountains so far formed in this collision.

Inside a mountain range

India (on the left) has pushed into Asia like a battering ram. The collision has hardly changed India, but Asia has buckled up and its crust has become almost twice as thick as it was before. This is partly a result of folding and fracturing of the Asian crust and partly due to masses of molten rock rising upward to add to the continental mass.

New oceanic crust is formed on the sea floor south of India

This fan-shaped wedge of sediment was scraped off the subducted plate and accreted, or joined, to Asia. It is known as an accretionary wedge.

Young sediments formed from erosion of Himalayan mountains

Old hard continental crust of India

The stark, glacier-hung peaks of Thamserku soar over the Everest region of Nepal.

The roof of the world

The Himalayan range includes the tallest mountain on Earth—Mount Everest—soaring to a height of 29,028 ft (8,848 m). Many other mountains in the range tower to heights of more than 26,240 ft (8,000 m). The exact height of Everest is difficult to determine. This is because the depth of the snow covering it changes all the time.

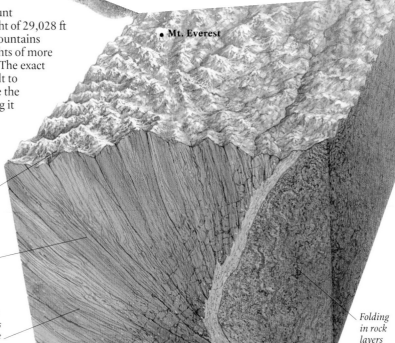

• Mt. Everest

Glaciers keep the mountain slopes steep

Fractures caused by crushing of rock layers

The youngest rocks of one slice are beside the oldest rocks of the next slice

Folding in rock layers

Himalayas cross section

The rocks that now make up the high mountain peaks of the Himalayas were formed on the floor of the Tethys Ocean, which once separated India and Asia. When the continents met, the heavy oceanic crust was subducted. But the lighter seafloor sediments were scraped off, one slice after another. Through folding and faulting, they became part of the Himalayan mountain range. Faults push one slice of rock over another. This close-up view of a section of the main illustration shows how the rock sequence created by faulting is repeated over and over again.

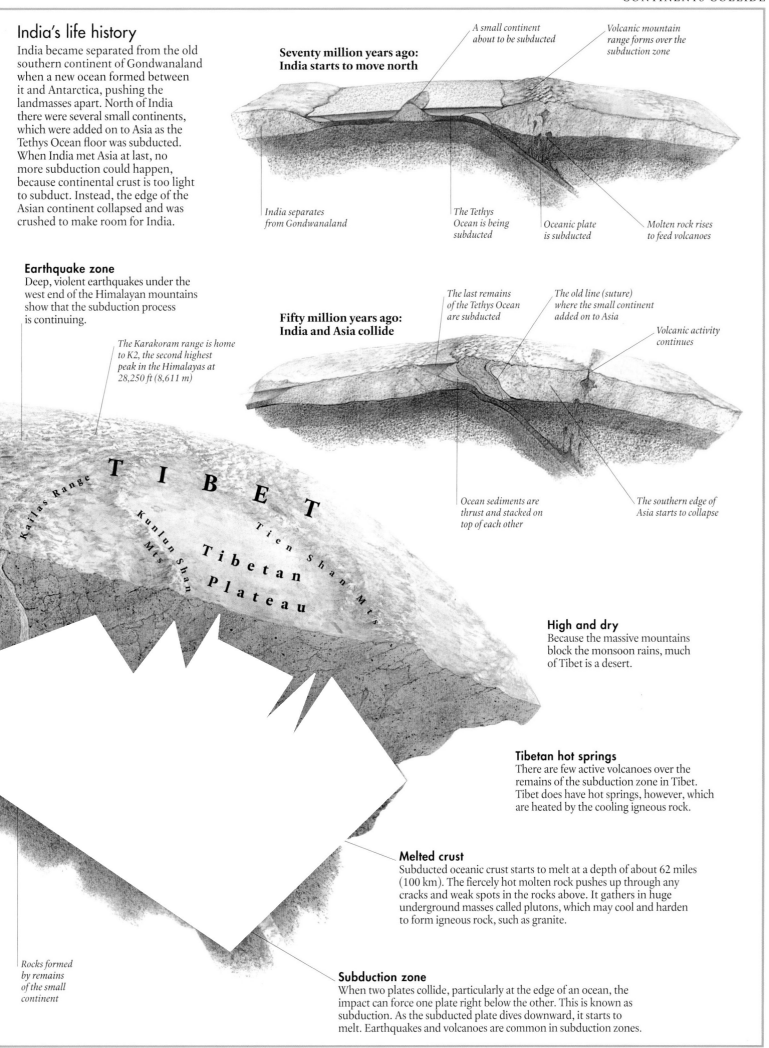

India's life history

India became separated from the old southern continent of Gondwanaland when a new ocean formed between it and Antarctica, pushing the landmasses apart. North of India there were several small continents, which were added on to Asia as the Tethys Ocean floor was subducted. When India met Asia at last, no more subduction could happen, because continental crust is too light to subduct. Instead, the edge of the Asian continent collapsed and was crushed to make room for India.

Seventy million years ago: India starts to move north

A small continent about to be subducted

Volcanic mountain range forms over the subduction zone

India separates from Gondwanaland

The Tethys Ocean is being subducted

Oceanic plate is subducted

Molten rock rises to feed volcanoes

Earthquake zone
Deep, violent earthquakes under the west end of the Himalayan mountains show that the subduction process is continuing.

The Karakoram range is home to K2, the second highest peak in the Himalayas at 28,250 ft (8,611 m)

Fifty million years ago: India and Asia collide

The last remains of the Tethys Ocean are subducted

The old line (suture) where the small continent added on to Asia

Volcanic activity continues

Ocean sediments are thrust and stacked on top of each other

The southern edge of Asia starts to collapse

TIBET

Tien Shan Mts

Kailas Range

Kunlun Shan Mts

Tibetan Plateau

High and dry
Because the massive mountains block the monsoon rains, much of Tibet is a desert.

Tibetan hot springs
There are few active volcanoes over the remains of the subduction zone in Tibet. Tibet does have hot springs, however, which are heated by the cooling igneous rock.

Melted crust
Subducted oceanic crust starts to melt at a depth of about 62 miles (100 km). The fiercely hot molten rock pushes up through any cracks and weak spots in the rocks above. It gathers in huge underground masses called plutons, which may cool and harden to form igneous rock, such as granite.

Rocks formed by remains of the small continent

Subduction zone
When two plates collide, particularly at the edge of an ocean, the impact can force one plate right below the other. This is known as subduction. As the subducted plate dives downward, it starts to melt. Earthquakes and volcanoes are common in subduction zones.

Making the Crust

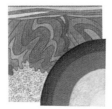

FORCES BOTH ABOVE and below the ground combine to create, destroy, and change the Earth's crust in a continual cycle. At spreading ridges, basaltic ocean crust is continually being made. This new crust moves away from the volcanic ridge, then plunges back into the Earth's interior at a subduction zone. Here, the oceanic crust melts into magma. This magma rises toward the surface either to feed a volcano or to form huge underground blobs called plutons. These may cool to make rocks such as granite, building the mountain range higher. Deep inside the mountain range, rocks are heated and recrystallized. As the mountains grow, the slopes are worn down and the loose rock fragments go to make new rocks. These processes form the Earth's three rock families: igneous, metamorphic, and sedimentary.

Galápagos
The Galápagos Islands are part of a spreading ridge southwest of Guatemala, in Central America.

The circles show how much of each of the three types of rocks—igneous, sedimentary, and metamorphic—is found in each region.

Creation and change
The coastal mountains of Guatemala and the neighboring Galápagos Islands are illustrated on these two pages. Some sections have been cut away to show the processes that create the Earth's crust. The mountain range, above a subduction zone, is made partly of granite and igneous rock made from melting of old oceanic crust. As the granite pushes toward the surface, old rocks that are caught up in mountain building are heated, compressed, and recrystallized to form metamorphic rocks.

Mountain rocks
In mountain regions, granites (igneous), sedimentary, and metamorphic rocks each make up about a third of all rock.

Coastal rocks
Huge amounts of sediment wear away from the nearby mountains and settle at the coastline. Only sedimentary rocks are found here.

A tor is a craggy hill formed from the erosion of granite. Vixen Tor (above) is in Devon, England.

Sierra Madre Mts

GUATEMALA

Granite landscape
The illustration below shows some features found in a granite landscape. The top of a batholith has been worn away, while nearby are the eroded roots of old volcanoes.

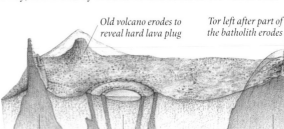

Old volcano erodes to reveal hard lava plug

Tor left after part of the batholith erodes

The rising blobs of magma are called plutons

Feeder pipe for a long-extinct, eroded volcano

Collapsed top of a granite pluton fills with water

Part of a huge dome-shaped granite batholith

Range rocks
Inside a young mountain range, almost all the rocks are either igneous or metamorphic rocks.

Granite batholith
A pluton cools slowly over many millions of years to form granite. New blobs of magma may remelt granite that has already cooled.

Basaltic landscape

The illustration on the right shows some of the features of a typical basaltic landscape. Flows of basalt lava spill downhill, over older flows now cracked into columns. On flat land, the lava spreads out in sheets, which may build up in layers. The upper parts of a lava flow are usually covered in blocklike lumps of lava. These weather away relatively quickly, forming a rich soil, which may be reddish in color.

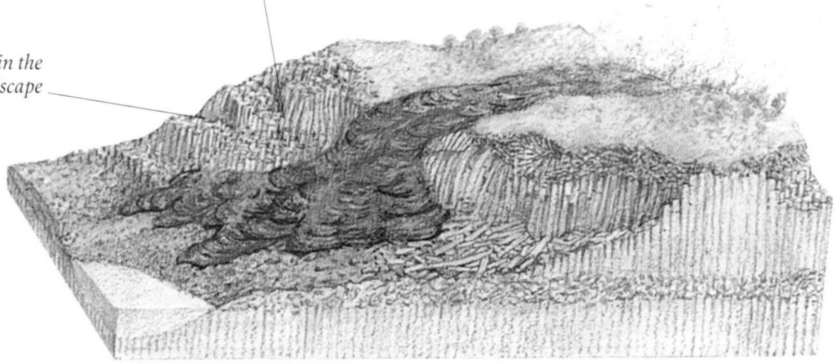

These tall basalt columns formed when the inside of an old lava flow slowly cooled and shrank, cracking into pencil shapes

Step in the landscape

Lava flows

A new lava flow cascades over the cliff of basalt columns. The molten lava moves inside a wrinkled skin of cooler lava, at a speed of up to 30 mph (50 km/h). As it cools, the lava slows down.

Crust destroyed

At a subduction zone, such as the Middle America Trench, basaltic oceanic crust goes back into the Earth's mantle. The sediments on top of the crust may be scraped off to join the edge of the continent.

Ridge rocks

At spreading ridges, almost all of the rock is igneous, with some sedimentary rock.

New sea floor at spreading ridge

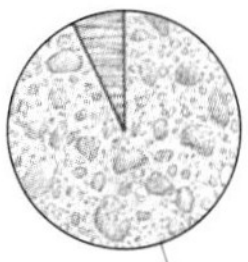

Island rocks

On volcanic islands, most of the rock is igneous, but there is some sedimentary rock to be found.

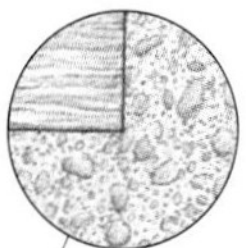

Basalt islands

The Galápagos Islands are built by basaltic rocks, made near the spreading ridge by hot magma rising from the mantle.

PACIFIC OCEAN

COLON RIDGE

GALÁPAGOS ISLANDS

MIDDLE AMERICA TRENCH

At spreading ridges, basaltic magma wells up to the surface and crystallizes. Layers of lava spill out on the ocean floor, making new crust, while some magma cools below.

Basaltic rocks go into the mantle and start to remelt at 62 miles (100 km) down

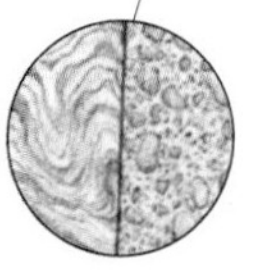

Clouds of ash and dust are thrown into the atmosphere

Ash and grains of rock are dumped in layers

A volcano erupts lava and ash

Igneous rock is weathered and eroded

Igneous rock
Extrusive igneous rock forms when erupted lava cools

Some sedimentary and metamorphic rock wears away to form new layers

These layers are squeezed and hardened into rock

The rock cycle

The rock cycle is how rocks change, one into another. A simple diagram of the cycle is shown on the right. Igneous rocks, for example, form when magma cools underground. They can also form when lava spilled out of a volcano cools on the surface. Igneous rocks are eroded and weathered to make layered sedimentary rocks. In mountain ranges, rock changes due to heat and pressure and recrystallizes to become metamorphic rock. There is no beginning or end to the cycle, and each transformation may take many millions of years.

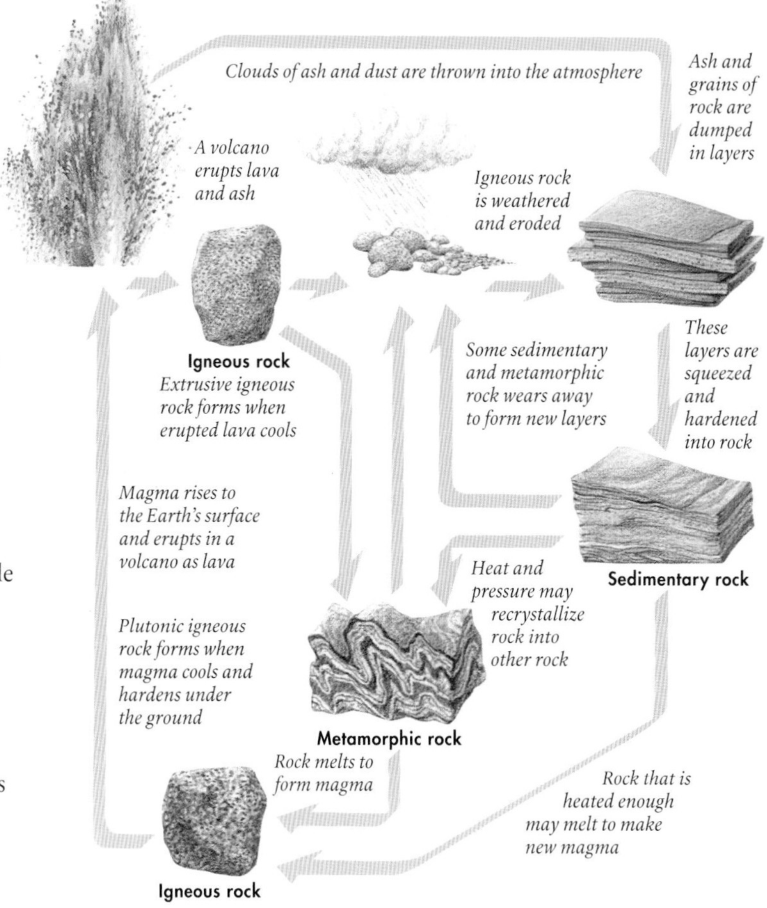

Magma rises to the Earth's surface and erupts in a volcano as lava

Plutonic igneous rock forms when magma cools and hardens under the ground

Sedimentary rock

Heat and pressure may recrystallize rock into other rock

Metamorphic rock
Rock melts to form magma

Rock that is heated enough may melt to make new magma

Igneous rock

Edge rocks

Found at the edge of the continent are igneous rocks, and metamorphic rocks that are made from them.

The Crust Wears Down

As NEW CRUST is created, forces act upon it all the time to wear it down again. Where surface rocks come into contact with the atmosphere, changes in the weather bring continual fluctuations in temperature and dampness. The rocks expand and contract and are waterlogged and dried out. These changes separate the mineral grains that make up the rocks, creating many tiny rock fragments. They may remain in place or may be carried away by rain, by melting snow and ice, by the wind, or by rivers, such as China's mighty Huang He seen here. Plant roots play their part by wedging rocks apart along cracks, allowing water to penetrate more deeply. Weathering is the chemical and physical breakdown of the rocks, and erosion is the removal and transport of rock grains.

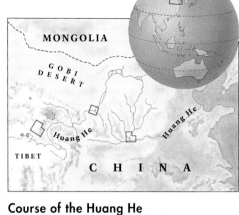

Course of the Huang He

The Huang He (Yellow River) of China travels 3,000 miles (4,830 km), from its source in the mountains of northern Tibet, through a loop near Mongolia, then south to the Yellow Sea.

Turning yellow

The river water is clear in the rocky mountains. But the soft yellow silt of the loess is easily washed away, especially from plowed fields. Here, the river picks up the bulk of the yellow sediments that give it its name.

The Huang He is so loaded with yellow silt; it is the same color as the silt of the river banks.

Meandering to the sea

Nearer to the sea, the river travels over the gentle slopes of the flood plain. By this point, the river is loaded with yellow sediments. As it meanders across the land here, it drops much of its load of silt. The river flows between banks made of silt that has already been deposited.

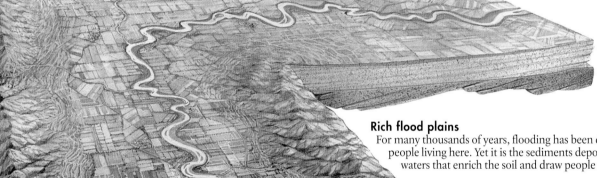

When it leaves the loess lands, almost a third of the river's total volume is sediment

Rich flood plains

For many thousands of years, flooding has been disastrous to the people living here. Yet it is the sediments deposited by the flood waters that enrich the soil and draw people to the area.

Slower-flowing river drops its load of sediment

Old layers of silt and gravel are laid one beside another on the inside of the bend

A curving course

As water rounds a curve in the river course, it flows fastest on the outside of the bend. The river is also deepest here. On the inside, the water is shallower and flows more slowly, so silt and pebbles are dropped. Over time, the riverbed moves outward, making a gentle bend into a sharp curve. In this way, the course of the river moves sideways as it snakes across flat land.

Fast-flowing water on the outside of the bend

Deeper water erodes the sand and gravel banks

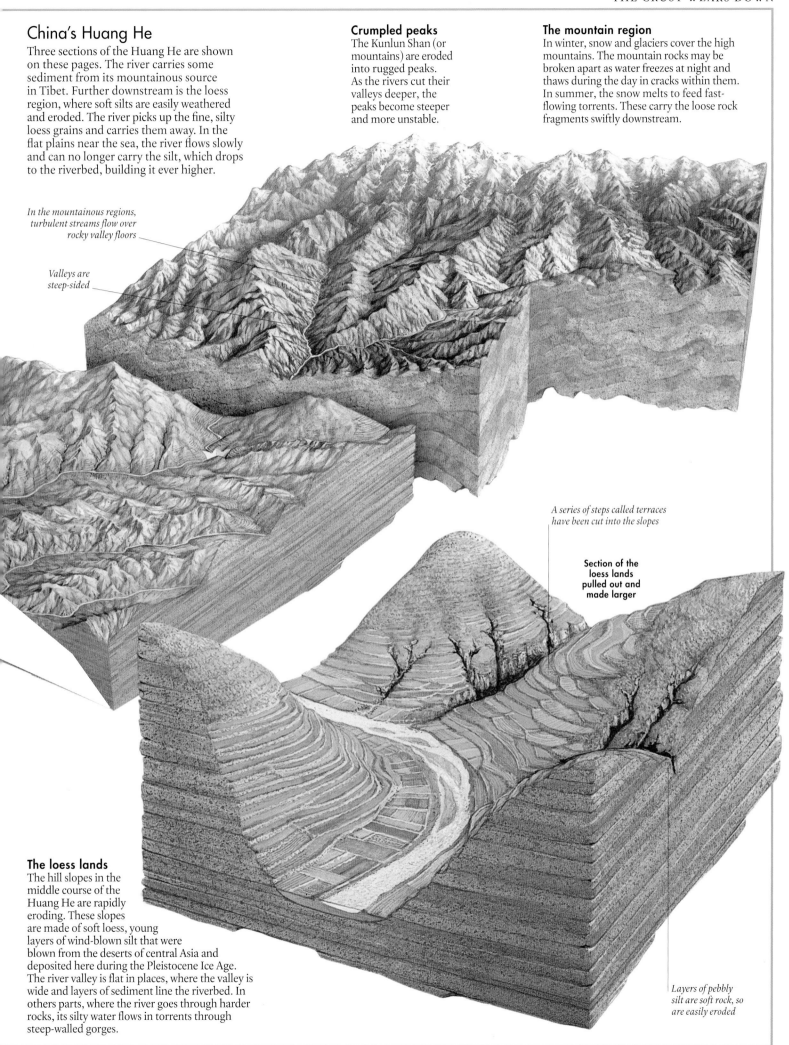

China's Huang He

Three sections of the Huang He are shown on these pages. The river carries some sediment from its mountainous source in Tibet. Further downstream is the loess region, where soft silts are easily weathered and eroded. The river picks up the fine, silty loess grains and carries them away. In the flat plains near the sea, the river flows slowly and can no longer carry the silt, which drops to the riverbed, building it ever higher.

In the mountainous regions, turbulent streams flow over rocky valley floors

Valleys are steep-sided

Crumpled peaks
The Kunlun Shan (or mountains) are eroded into rugged peaks. As the rivers cut their valleys deeper, the peaks become steeper and more unstable.

The mountain region
In winter, snow and glaciers cover the high mountains. The mountain rocks may be broken apart as water freezes at night and thaws during the day in cracks within them. In summer, the snow melts to feed fast-flowing torrents. These carry the loose rock fragments swiftly downstream.

A series of steps called terraces have been cut into the slopes

Section of the loess lands pulled out and made larger

The loess lands
The hill slopes in the middle course of the Huang He are rapidly eroding. These slopes are made of soft loess, young layers of wind-blown silt that were blown from the deserts of central Asia and deposited here during the Pleistocene Ice Age. The river valley is flat in places, where the valley is wide and layers of sediment line the riverbed. In others parts, where the river goes through harder rocks, its silty water flows in torrents through steep-walled gorges.

Layers of pebbly silt are soft rock, so are easily eroded

31

Layering the Land

THE SEDIMENT CARRIED by rivers and glaciers from mountain regions eventually finds a resting place. This might be as boulders and gravel at the foot of a mountain, dunes in a desert, silt and salt in a desert lake, or sand or pebbles on a riverbank or coastline. Sediments are laid down in layers. These layers are exposed to view where they have been uplifted and then cut through by eroding rivers. Perhaps the most spectacular example on Earth is the immensely deep Grand Canyon, carved into the layered rocks of the Colorado Plateau by the Colorado River.

This spectacular view of the Grand Canyon was taken from Mather Point on the South Rim.

Bright Angel Point

North Rim
More than 1,000 ft (300 m) higher than the South Rim, the North Rim is covered with snow until late spring.

Canyon colors
The different types of rocks give the canyon its spectacular colors, from gray limestone and yellow sandstone to pink granite and dark schist.

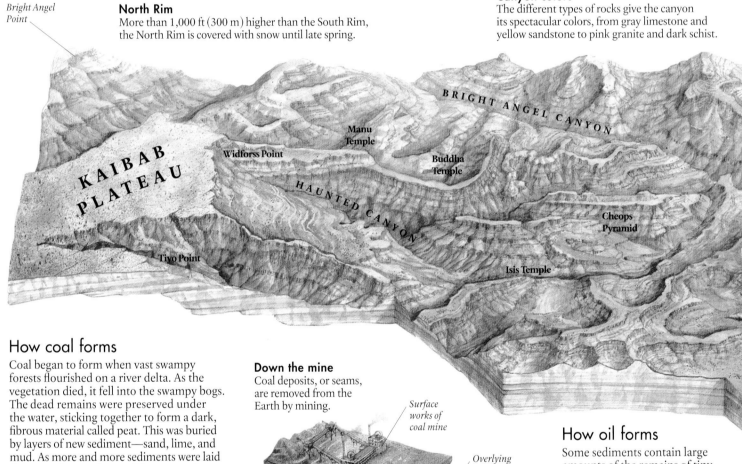

KAIBAB PLATEAU

Widforss Point

Manu Temple

Buddha Temple

BRIGHT ANGEL CANYON

HAUNTED CANYON

Cheops Pyramid

Isis Temple

Tiyo Point

How coal forms
Coal began to form when vast swampy forests flourished on a river delta. As the vegetation died, it fell into the swampy bogs. The dead remains were preserved under the water, sticking together to form a dark, fibrous material called peat. This was buried by layers of new sediment—sand, lime, and mud. As more and more sediments were laid down, each peaty layer of forest remains became compressed. After many millions of years, the peat was compressed and heated to form coal.

Down the mine
Coal deposits, or seams, are removed from the Earth by mining.

Surface works of coal mine

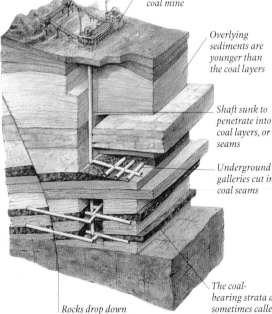

Overlying sediments are younger than the coal layers

Shaft sunk to penetrate into coal layers, or seams

Underground galleries cut into coal seams

Rocks drop down on this side of fault

The coal-bearing strata are sometimes called "coal measures"

How oil forms
Some sediments contain large amounts of the remains of tiny sea plants. When these are buried, they are "cooked" by heat and pressure to become oil.

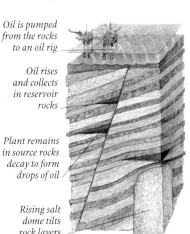

Oil is pumped from the rocks to an oil rig

Oil rises and collects in reservoir rocks

Plant remains in source rocks decay to form drops of oil

Rising salt dome tilts rock layers

Trees to peat
Soft vegetation that grows in a tropical swamp may form peat.

Peat to coal
Layer after layer of new sediment compresses the peat to coal.

Arizona's Grand Canyon and Colorado River
The Colorado River has carved the awesome Grand Canyon through Arizona, in the southwestern United States. The canyon is 217 miles (349 km) long, up to 19 miles (30 km) wide, and 1 mile (1.6 km) deep.

Changing sediments

As sea level changes with time, coastlines move. Sea level rises when spreading ridges are more active. The undersea mountains push aside ocean water so that it floods the continental shelves.

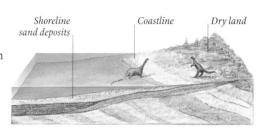

Changing shorelines

When sea level is lower, during an ice age, or when spreading ridges are less active, the continental shelves dry out. Shoreline sediments such as sand are then deposited on top of the older, deeper water sediments.

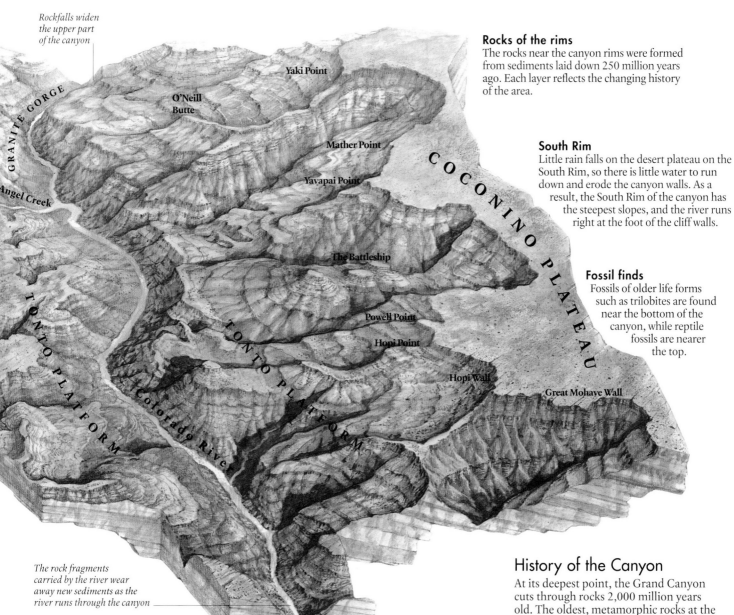

Rockfalls widen the upper part of the canyon

Yaki Point

O'Neill Butte

GRANITE GORGE

Angel Creek

Mather Point

Yavapai Point

The Battleship

Powell Point

Hopi Point

Hopi Wall

TONTO PLATFORM

Colorado River

TONTO PLATFORM

COCONINO PLATEAU

Great Mohave Wall

Rocks of the rims
The rocks near the canyon rims were formed from sediments laid down 250 million years ago. Each layer reflects the changing history of the area.

South Rim
Little rain falls on the desert plateau on the South Rim, so there is little water to run down and erode the canyon walls. As a result, the South Rim of the canyon has the steepest slopes, and the river runs right at the foot of the cliff walls.

Fossil finds
Fossils of older life forms such as trilobites are found near the bottom of the canyon, while reptile fossils are nearer the top.

The rock fragments carried by the river wear away new sediments as the river runs through the canyon

History of the Canyon

At its deepest point, the Grand Canyon cuts through rocks 2,000 million years old. The oldest, metamorphic rocks at the bottom of the gorge were formed as part of an ancient mountain range. Younger layers of limestone, shale, and sandstone were laid over these mountains, then lifted up into the Colorado Plateau. As the plateau rose and domed up in the middle, the river carved its course deeper, keeping pace with the uplift. The rocks of the canyon rim are about 250 million years old.

Deep cut
The rising plateau gave the river a steeper slope. This made it flow faster, so it had more energy to cut away its river bed and deepen the canyon floor.

Steep cut
The plateau's rapid uplift means the river has carved an even steeper canyon over the last two million years. In its long history, the canyon may never have been so impressive as it is today.

The Crust Changes

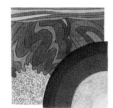

AT THE HEART of the Earth's mountain ranges lie rocks that are different from sedimentary and igneous rocks. They have unique textures and structures and contain new and different minerals. These are metamorphic rocks—igneous or sedimentary rocks that have been changed. The changes are brought about by heat given off by nearby igneous rock intrusions, by the immense pressure from the weight of the overlying mountains, or by chemical action.

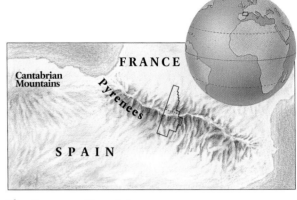

The Pyrenees Mountains

Forming a border between France and Spain 270 miles (435 km) long, the Pyrenees are one of the Earth's young, still growing, mountain ranges.

Metamorphic mountains

The Pyrenees mountain range, seen on these pages, has granite intrusions at its core. The hot, molten granite swelled upward, heating up the surrounding rocks and pushing them aside. Over many millions of years, the sedimentary rocks and older igneous rocks were metamorphosed within the mountain range. Today, many miles of rock have been eroded off the top of the Pyrenees, to reveal its metamorphic heart.

These layers of sedimentary rock at Pico de Vallibierna have been folded and overfolded until they are lying down, or recumbent.

Pico de Vallibierna, Spain

The folded rock pattern shown in the photograph on the left is outlined here.

Folding up rocks

In mountain ranges, the forces that made the mountains push and fold the sedimentary rock, which was first laid down in layers.

Change in the range

Metamorphism that happens over a wide area, especially in mountain ranges, is known as regional metamorphism.

Lago Helada, Spain

The outline shows a recumbent fold in the strata of Lago Helada, seen on the right. The folding is so intense that some of the layers are now upside down.

This icy lake in Spain's Ordesa National Park shows a reflection of the folded rocks of Lago Helada above.

Section through granite intrusion

Intrusion

This granite intrusion cooled many miles down in the crust.

200 million years ago
In the Tethys Ocean, sediments were laid down on the ocean bed and along its shorelines.

100 million years ago
Iberia and France crunched together, and a mountain range began to grow.

Iberian drift
As Africa moved northward, Iberia (the landmass of Spain and Portugal) crunched sideways against Europe. Layers of sediment from the old ocean floor were probably scraped up and were later eroded away, so there is no record left of their existence.

History of the Pyrenees
A hundred million years ago, the great Tethys Ocean stretched between Europe and Africa. As immense forces in the Earth pushed Africa northward, the ocean was swallowed at a subduction zone. Sediments from the ocean floor were buckled and crushed, and intensely overfolded, as great rock masses were pushed one over another to make the Pyrenees.

Rocks are folded and pushed one over another

Two million years ago
Older granite pushed up into the folded and crushed rocks, complicating the mountain range even more. All the rocks were heated and metamorphosed.

Rocks nearest the intrusion are heated the most

Old granite intrusion deep within the mountains

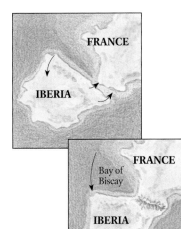

FRANCE

IBERIA

FRANCE

Bay of Biscay

IBERIA

Shared history
The Pyrenees are among the world's youngest mountain chains, the same age as the Alps and Carpathians in Europe and the Himalayas in Asia.

Rock that formed many miles deep has been worn from the peaks

Foothills
The rocks of the foothills show less complicated folding and less intense metamorphism.

Folded and metamorphosed rocks near the granite

The dark rock at the center of Pic la Canau has eroded more easily, making a gully on the slope.

Pic la Canau, France
The outline shows how the rock was stretched and cracked over the top of the fold, allowing erosion to bite in. The top of the fold has all worn away.

HOW ROCKS CHANGE
As rocks are compressed and heated, their mineral grains gradually rearrange themselves in response to the changing pressure and temperature. Atoms move from places where pressure is greatest to the places where it is less intense. New minerals grow that are stable at high pressures and temperatures. The type of metamorphic rock that forms depends on the composition of the original rock and how much heat or pressure—or both—brings about the change.

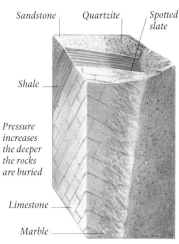

Sandstone *Quartzite* *Spotted slate*

Shale

Pressure increases the deeper the rocks are buried

Limestone

Marble

Heat radiates outward from the granite intrusion

35

Amazing Earth

EARTH'S LANDSCAPES show an amazing variety, from deserts or spectacular waterfalls to the polar ice regions or graceful volcano cones. Each is the result of a unique geological history. Some landscapes are the result of recent erosion or tectonic (building) processes, which in the vast time scale of Earth's history means changes over the last few tens of millions of years. Others were sculpted by the same processes but have been little changed for hundreds of millions of years.

Canadian tundra

In summer, soggy plains stretch in all directions in the Arctic regions of northern Canada and Siberia. Below the surface, the ground is permanently frozen, so the summer meltwater collects in swampy pools. At the end of the summer, these pools of water freeze again. When water just beneath the surface expands to form ice, it may push the soil up into small domes called pingoes.

These red sandstone towers are the North and South Mittens.

Monument Valley, Utah

The large mesas and smaller buttes that tower over Monument Valley are isolated flat-topped mountains, made of horizontal layers of sedimentary rock. Over hundreds of thousands of years, they have worn away, leaving behind tall towers of rock.

Loose rock collects at the base of the hoodoos

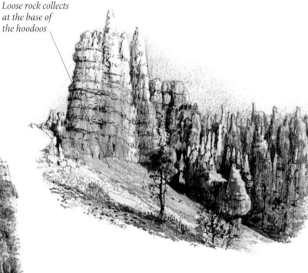

Bryce Canyon, Utah

The hoodoos of Bryce Canyon are a mass of pinnacles sculpted from layers of soft young rock. The canyon's pinky-orange limestone is sediment that collected in a lake 60 million years ago. Weather has worn the rocks into colorful hoodoos.

Angel Falls, Venezuela

The waterfall with the longest drop in the world tumbles 3,212 ft (979 m) off the wet swamplands of a plateau called Auyán Tepuí in Venezuela. The water changes into white mist before reaching the bottom.

Antarctic ice cap

A vast sheet of ice makes the cold deserts of Antarctica. The ice cap has formed from snow that has accumulated over tens of thousands of years. The ice is over 14,760 ft (4,500 m) thick in places. Only the tallest summits of the Transantarctic Mountains break through the ice.

The ice cap contains 90 percent of all the ice on Earth.

Tundra

NORTH AMERICA

Bryce Canyon •
• Monument Valley

Tropic of Cancer

ATLANTIC

Angel Falls •

Equator

SOUTH AMERICA

PACIFIC OCEAN

Tropic of Capricorn

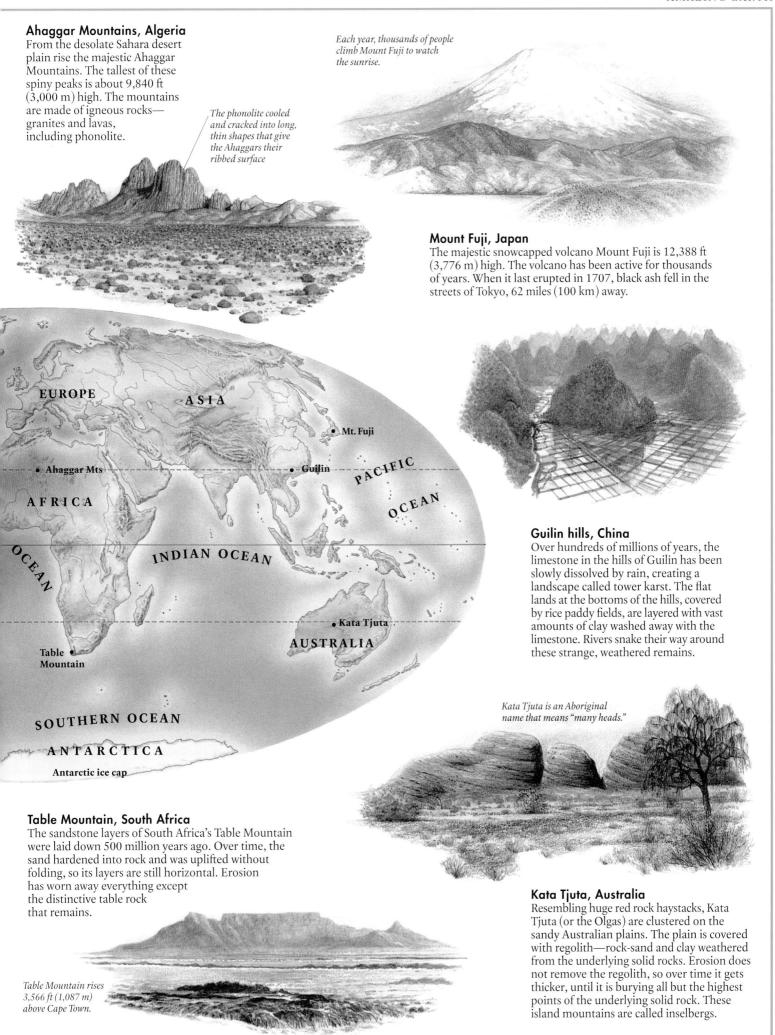

Ahaggar Mountains, Algeria

From the desolate Sahara desert plain rise the majestic Ahaggar Mountains. The tallest of these spiny peaks is about 9,840 ft (3,000 m) high. The mountains are made of igneous rocks— granites and lavas, including phonolite.

The phonolite cooled and cracked into long, thin shapes that give the Ahaggars their ribbed surface

Each year, thousands of people climb Mount Fuji to watch the sunrise.

Mount Fuji, Japan

The majestic snowcapped volcano Mount Fuji is 12,388 ft (3,776 m) high. The volcano has been active for thousands of years. When it last erupted in 1707, black ash fell in the streets of Tokyo, 62 miles (100 km) away.

Guilin hills, China

Over hundreds of millions of years, the limestone in the hills of Guilin has been slowly dissolved by rain, creating a landscape called tower karst. The flat lands at the bottoms of the hills, covered by rice paddy fields, are layered with vast amounts of clay washed away with the limestone. Rivers snake their way around these strange, weathered remains.

Kata Tjuta is an Aboriginal name that means "many heads."

Table Mountain, South Africa

The sandstone layers of South Africa's Table Mountain were laid down 500 million years ago. Over time, the sand hardened into rock and was uplifted without folding, so its layers are still horizontal. Erosion has worn away everything except the distinctive table rock that remains.

Table Mountain rises 3,566 ft (1,087 m) above Cape Town.

Kata Tjuta, Australia

Resembling huge red rock haystacks, Kata Tjuta (or the Olgas) are clustered on the sandy Australian plains. The plain is covered with regolith—rock-sand and clay weathered from the underlying solid rocks. Erosion does not remove the regolith, so over time it gets thicker, until it is burying all but the highest points of the underlying solid rock. These island mountains are called inselbergs.

Map labels
EUROPE
ASIA
Mt. Fuji
Ahaggar Mts
Guilin
PACIFIC
AFRICA
OCEAN
OCEAN
INDIAN OCEAN
Kata Tjuta
AUSTRALIA
Table Mountain
SOUTHERN OCEAN
ANTARCTICA
Antarctic ice cap

Planet Water

OCEAN WATERS COVER almost three-quarters of Earth's surface. The largest ocean, the Pacific, is also the oldest and is about one-third of the Earth's entire surface. Around its fringes lie the deepest places on the Earth's surface, the great ocean trenches. Some trenches are much deeper even than the mountains on land are high. The ocean floor is studded with volcanoes and flat-topped mountains and is crisscrossed by the world's largest mountain chain. Layers of sediment carpet the entire deep ocean floor. Shallow water surrounds each continent; these continental shelves are the flooded margins of the continents.

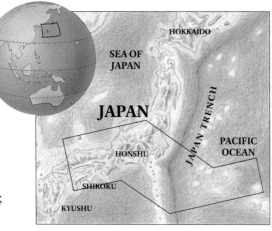

Japan trench

Japan lies on an active continental margin, where the Pacific Ocean plate is being subducted underneath Japan. The deep Japan Trench shown on these pages marks the place where the ocean floor plunges beneath its neighboring plate. As the plate jolts underneath, earthquakes are generated.

Young mountains

High mountains with steep slopes make up much of Japan's landscape. The young mountain rocks erode rapidly, pouring loose sediment into the ocean.

Islands of Japan

Japan is a chain of islands east of Asia. A deep ocean trench lies along its Pacific coast, and a small young ocean separates it from mainland Asia.

At the edge of the continent

The continental slope stretches from the edge of the continental shelf all the way down to the ocean deep. It is covered with layers of mud and sand eroded away from the nearby continent.

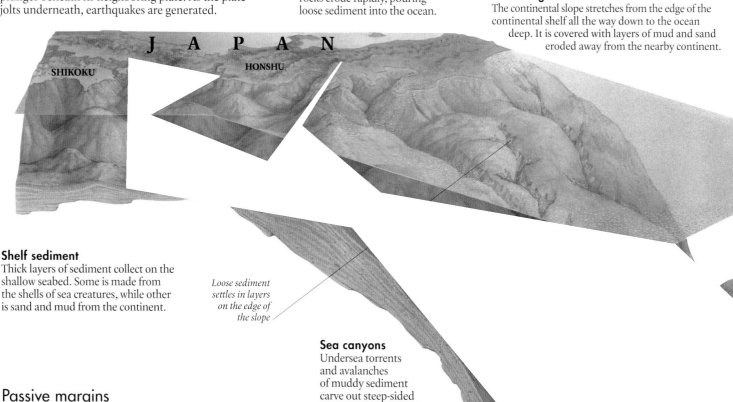

Shelf sediment

Thick layers of sediment collect on the shallow seabed. Some is made from the shells of sea creatures, while other is sand and mud from the continent.

Loose sediment settles in layers on the edge of the slope

Sea canyons

Undersea torrents and avalanches of muddy sediment carve out steep-sided canyons into the depths of the trench.

Passive margins

The continental shelves fringing most land areas in the Atlantic Ocean are wide and shallow. They are known as passive margins. As Europe and the Americas split and the ocean between them grew, the continental edge was pushed from the spreading ridge. Much of the continental shelf was flooded at the end of the Ice Age.

An old deposit of sediment from the coastal water

Ocean trench

A trench is deep and narrow, with steep walls. Some of the sediment that collects here is carried back into the Earth with the subducting plate.

Passive margins have no subduction zone, and few earthquakes

Continental slope ends at a pile of sediment called the continental rise

Continental shelf is part of the neighboring continent

Land hemisphere

Although Africa, Asia, and Europe dominate this view of the globe, they are surrounded by the Atlantic, Indian, and Southern Oceans. The Atlantic and the Southern Oceans have been growing larger over the past 200 million years, as the continents have drifted apart. At the same time, an old ocean that once separated the northern and southern continents has shrunk to become the Mediterranean Sea.

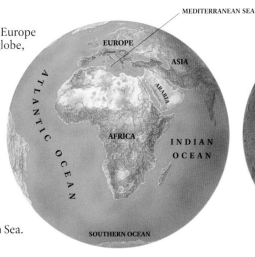

Ocean hemisphere

The Pacific Ocean is so vast it extends across a whole hemisphere, stretching nearly halfway around the globe at its widest point. Within the Pacific is the lowest point on Earth—the Mariana Trench, 35,826 ft (10,920 m) deep. Although subduction has been swallowing the ocean crust along its margins for many tens of millions of years, the spreading ridges to the south and east of the ocean, where new crust is formed, are keeping pace.

Shrinking sea

The Aral Sea is a landlocked salty lake in west Asia. Once the world's fourth-largest lake, it is now one-tenth the size. Its waters were diverted for irrigation in the 1960s. As it got shallower, water evaporated faster and what remained was too salty to support life. In 2014, the eastern lake dried up completely, but reflowing efforts helped revive the lake and the fishing industry in the north.

This satellite image shows the extent of the Aral Sea in 1973.

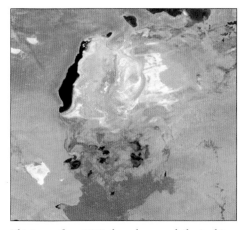

This image from 2019 shows how much the Aral Sea has shrunk.

Undersea volcanoes
Volcanoes pepper the ocean floor. Some are active and grow large enough to rise above the water, forming islands.

Guyots
A guyot is a sunken flat-topped mountain. Guyots were once islands, but their tops were worn flat by pounding waves. They sank under the sea as the seafloor subsided.

Age of the seafloor
The ocean floor being subducted under Japan today is about 200 million years old. It was once part of Panthalassa, a massive ocean nearly twice the size of the Pacific that surrounded Pangaea.

Ocean depths

Depth in feet/meters	
Euphotic ("good light") zone	0
Disphotic ("bad light") zone	740 ft (226 m)
	3,300 ft (1,000 m)
Aphotic ("no light") zone	
Seabed	

Sunlight penetrates only the euphotic and disphotic zones. The oxygen-rich water supports a vast range of life. The aphotic zone is inky black with cold waters and immense pressure—few life forms can survive here.

Deep-sea sediments
Different types of sediment collect on the deep-sea floor. Gray-brown muddy sediment from land is shaped into mounds by ocean currents. The abyssal ocean floor is covered with red-brown clay and manganese nodules. White-gray lime-rich ooze covers the crest of seamounts.

Final resting place
Buried in the deep sea sediment are whale ear bones, skeletons of microscopic creatures—even bits of meteorites from space.

The Ocean Floor

RISING FROM THE DEEP OCEAN FLOOR are the longest mountain chains on Earth. These are the spreading ridges, where magma oozes up to form new oceanic crust. The ocean floor today is the youngest part of the Earth's crust. It has all formed over the last 200 million years. No older ocean crust is left, because it has all been swallowed back into the mantle. New crust is made at cracks in the spreading ridges. When the crust beneath the cracks stretches, rift valleys form. As the continents on either side of the rift valley move farther apart, there is continually space for more and more new crust. Tall chimney stacks called black smokers billow thick black clouds along cooler parts of the spreading ridge.

Ridges and rift valleys

A section of the vast underwater mountain chain that snakes through the Atlantic Ocean, the Mid-Atlantic Ridge, is shown here. Its massive peaks rise up to 13,123 ft (4,000 m) above the ocean floor. The rift valley at the center of the ridge is where the seafloor is spreading. Several black smokers dot the middle of the valley. A section of the rift valley is pulled out and shown larger, to reveal its structure.

Faults

As the growing ocean floor stretches, it cracks along lines (faults) more or less parallel to the rift valley. Steep cliffs along the fault lines gradually grow less steep as blocks of rock fall down to the bottom.

Each section of ocean floor breaks along a sloping fault, so its layers become tilted

Pillow lava

Magma oozing up from the mantle becomes basalt lava, a dark-colored rock rich in iron and magnesium. When the hot lava cools in contact with sea water, it makes lumpy round shapes called pillow lava.

Dykes

Under the pillows is a layer of vertical dykes, where magma crystallized as it came up through the rift valley crack.

The rising cloud of water looks black because of the minerals it contains

Black smokers

These tall stacks are made of mineral deposits. The black "smoke" they belch out is actually tiny grains of metal sulfides. Originally, the sulfides were in the new rocks of the ocean floor. As ocean water seeps through cracks in the cooling rock, it dissolves the sulfides. Hot magma below the center of the rift makes this water boil. As the water bubbles up through the cracks, it deposits the sulfides and other minerals to build chimneys up to 33 ft (10 m) tall.

A black smoker grows when the boiling water shooting from a crack meets the cold water near the seafloor

The chimneys are brittle and may break off, leaving heaps of broken fragments around the smokers

40

Mid-Atlantic Ridge

Two hundred million years ago, there was no ocean between Europe and Africa, and the Americas. Then a crack developed that grew and widened, and new ocean crust filled in the gaps along the Mid-Atlantic Ridge to form the Atlantic Ocean. By dating ocean-bed rocks, scientists know that the oldest oceanic crust is nearest the continents, and "stripes" of ocean floor are younger the nearer they are to the still-active ridge. The map on the right shows the age of the crust in each of its sections.

The longest mountains on Earth

The Mid-Atlantic Ridge stretches 7,000 miles (11,300 km) from Iceland in the north to the edge of the Southern Ocean in the south.

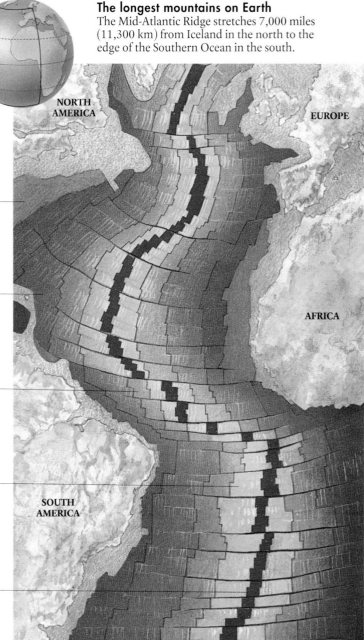

NORTH AMERICA

EUROPE

AFRICA

SOUTH AMERICA

Transform faults

The spreading ridges are in short sections across the oceans. Every few tens of miles the active part of the ridge is moved sideways by fractures called transform faults. These cut right across the middle of the ridge and offset the crust into sections.

The fractures extend far beyond the transform fault, where they offset the spreading ridge

200 million years ago (mya)
The oldest crust is nearest the land.

66–145 mya
The crust here formed in the age of dinosaurs.

23–66 mya
The Pyrenees and Himalayas grew as this crust formed.

2.5–23 mya
The Himalayas soared higher as this crust formed.

0–2.5 mya
The youngest crust is nearest the ridge.

Birth of the Red Sea

The Red Sea in eastern Africa formed in the same way as the Atlantic Ocean—at a spreading ridge. Today it is only about 186 miles (300 km) across, but millions of years from now it may rival the Atlantic in size. The Red Sea was born 20 million years ago as Arabia started to crack away from Africa. Magma rose up and great amounts of basalt lava poured out over the land. Later eruptions concentrated in the center part of the widening rift. This eventually became the ocean floor when sea water entered the valley.

Lifting the crust
Cracks develop as magma pushes up against the overlying continental crust, stretching and lifting it upward.

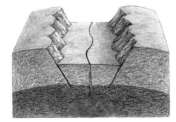

Rift valley forms
The continent begins to crack apart, and a central block sinks, forming a rift valley. Magma squeezes in to fill the cracks.

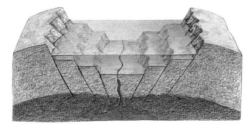

From valley to sea
Fresh cracks fringe the widening rift valley as its walls move farther apart. Sea water enters the deep basin.

The Life of a River

A TINY TORRENT OF WATER high up in the mountains eventually becomes a vast, placid river flowing into the sea, but it has to go through several stages and pass through many landscapes before it gets there. Streams and rivers are fed from water that runs over the surface of the ground as well as from underground water seeping out from the rock. In the great continents, rivers usually rise in mountains near one coastline. Some travel vast distances across ancient routes to a far coastline; others take their water to inland lakes or seas. The river shown on these pages is the Nile—the longest river in the world.

Course of the Nile
The Nile River flows 4,145 miles (6,670 km) northward through the Sahara Desert to the Mediterranean Sea. The shorter route eastward to the Red Sea is blocked by a range of mountains that are younger than the river course.

Birth of a river

In mountain regions where there is plenty of rain and melting snow, rivers are turbulent. Many little rivulets flow over steep rocky landscapes, carving their pathway as they go. Some mountain ranges today are slowly growing higher. River valleys in these growing mountains stay steep and full of waterfalls. The rising mountains ensure plenty of rain and snow falls from cooling weather clouds to keep the rivers flowing.

Lake Victoria
Lake Victoria is the source of the upper valley of the Nile River. It lies on a recently uplifted plateau.

Kabalega Falls
The river plunges more than 130 ft (39 m) downward over a steep, clifflike waterfall, surrounded by the rising mountains of Uganda.

Rapids
A hard, rocky riverbed creates a series of rapids where the water tumbles in all directions as it rushes over the rocks.

Swamps
The Nile flows sluggishly through the reed swamps of the Sudd region.

River junction
The two main branches of the river—the White Nile and the Blue Nile—join near the town of Khartoum in Sudan.

Deep plunge pool at base of waterfall

The way to the sea

The steepest part of a river's course is usually near its source in the mountains. The closer the river gets to the sea, the flatter its pathway becomes. But along the route, there may be many interruptions to this gradual change in slope. These might be lakes, where the river slowly fills in a hollow with pebbles, sand, and mud. Waterfalls form where the river runs over bands of hard rock onto softer rock.

Ancient river valleys
During the Ice Age, the climate here was wetter. Rivers from mountains near the Red Sea ran into the Nile. Today, these dried-up river valleys are called wadis.

Tributaries
The Blue Nile brings water from the Ethiopian mountains, which are hit by heavy seasonal rains. The White Nile carries water from eastern Africa. Smaller rivers that join a main river are called tributaries.

GRAND CANYON OF THE NILE RIVER

Overall, the slope of a river's course relates to the sea level at the time. Five million years ago, the Mediterranean Sea dried up so that sea level, as far as the Mediterranean rivers were concerned, was 6,560 ft (2,000 m) lower than it is today. At this time, the Nile cut its pathway down to meet this deeper level. Sand and gravel carried by the river scoured away at the layers of rock, forming a steep-sided canyon.

The Nile canyon, which may have looked similar to America's Grand Canyon, extended more than 620 miles (1,000 km) to Aswan. Over time, the sea level rose again, and the river dropped its sediment to fill in the canyon.

Five million years ago
The Mediterranean dried up and sea level was lower. The Nile carved a deep canyon, to try to meet the new sea level.

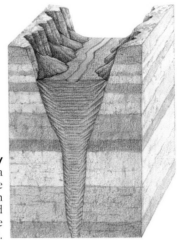

Present day
Later, when the sea level rose again, the canyon slowly filled in with gravel, sand, and mud from higher up the river's course.

Meanders

Where the river course runs through flat land, its path winds along in broad curves. These are called meanders. The meander curves continually get bigger and wider. This is because the water travels fastest around the outside of the curve, cutting its pathway through the river banks. On the inside of the curve, the water travels more slowly. Here it drops the sediment it is carrying, and forms a beach. When it is in flood, a river can cut right through the narrow neck of land between meanders, straightening its course. The curving lake left behind is called an oxbow. An oxbow lake gradually silts up, as it is no longer part of the river.

The Okavango River meanders through Botswana on its way to its outlet in the Okavanga Delta.

Deltas

Rivers in flood carry along huge amounts of gravel, sand, and mud. When a river reaches the relatively calm sea water, it drops its load of sediment in layers. These layers cannot build up unless the region is sinking. Instead they get carried farther out to sea. In this way, the river may build up a triangular-shaped area of new, swampy land, crisscrossed by small channels of water. This is called a delta, after the Greek letter "delta" (Δ), which is a triangle.

The Nile Delta
The Nile River divides into many sluggish rivers (distributaries) that wander over the enlarging fan of the delta region in Egypt.

Sahara Desert
The Nile finds its pathway through 1,700 miles (2,375 km) of the Sahara Desert on its journey to the Mediterranean Sea. It rains very rarely in the Sahara, so there are no tributary rivers on this part of the Nile.

Flood waters
On the broad, low-lying plain, flood water from the Nile has spread onto the land at either side, forming a strip of green, fertile land in the midst of the brown desert.

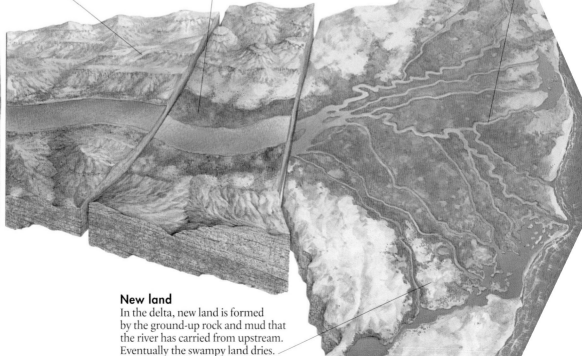

Cataracts
Where the river passes over hard granite rocks, it forms great foaming rapids of white water. These are known as cataracts. There are six cataracts on the Nile.

New land
In the delta, new land is formed by the ground-up rock and mud that the river has carried from upstream. Eventually the swampy land dries.

Coastlines

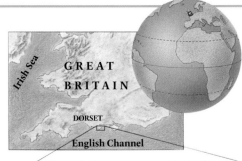

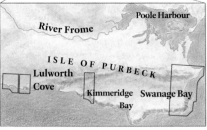

WHERE SEA MEETS LAND, the battle between the pounding waves and solid rock creates the Earth's changing coastlines. The water of the seas and oceans is continually moving, driven by the energy of waves and currents. As the waves crash one after another against the shoreline, they find any weaknesses in the rock and wear their way through. Bays, for example, are carved out where coastal rock is softer. Even cliffs made of harder rocks are undercut by waves. Once undermined, the cliff breaks away in occasional rockfalls. The sea builds as well as destroys. Eroded rock pieces are sorted out by waves, the smaller ones carried away while larger pieces stay put to build a beach. Sand and pebbles can also add new fingerlike land to the coastline. The illustrations on these pages show how the sea is continually remodeling the coastline of Dorset, England.

England's Dorset coastline

Dorset is a county in southwestern England. Its coastline stretches along the English Channel, which separates Britain from France. The area of Dorset seen on these pages is called the Isle of Purbeck.

Rocky walls

Some coasts are bordered by hard, rocky walls of granite or limestone. These are strong enough to resist waves and slow down the rate of erosion.

Bat's Head

Durdle Door

Man O' War Cove

Spit and tombolo

A long ridge of sand or pebbles that extends from the land into open water is called a spit. The sand is carried by drifting waves and dropped. A tombolo is a spit between an island and land.

Spit

Stair Hole

Lulworth Cove

Softer clay rocks behind the wall

Hard band of limestone makes a vertical wall

Hole in the roof

Waves can pound into cracks in the rock, pushing out the air inside so a spray of water rises from the rock with each wave.

Coastal rocks

The underlying rock shows why the Dorset coast has worn into an irregular shape. Headlands are found where the rock is more resistant, while bays are sculpted out of softer rock.

Kimmeridge Bay

Sea finds a weak spot in the wall and starts to eat through

A second weak spot

Waves swirl into the cove and wear away its sides

Soft rocks are easily eroded and are etched away by waves to form a cove

Alternating layers of hard limestone and soft clay support a series of ledges stretching out to sea

The eroded rock is deposited in the bay to form a beach

Bites from the land

The pounding waves can wear away the land one bite at a time. Once the hard wall of rock is cut through by the waves, the softer rocks behind are easily worn away. First a small cove is carved out, with the sea swirling in at high tide. The waves wear away the sides of the cove, enlarging it to make a curved bay.

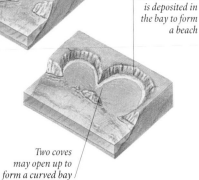

Two coves may open up to form a curved bay

The Dorset coast

The Dorset coastline is built layer by layer of soft and hard rocks that have been gently folded. The folding has broken up some of the harder rocks, making them more easily eroded by waves pounding against the coast. Other hard rock layers form walls able to resist the waves. The soft rocks make up low ground, which is easily invaded by the sea. Dorset's beaches are made of hard, flinty pebbles called shingle. As waves break onto the shingle, their energy is absorbed in rolling the pebbles, protecting the cliffs and landscape from being worn away.

44

Longshore drift

Each incoming wave breaks at an angle to the shore. The surf picks up pebbles and sand and moves them slightly sideways up the beach, then gravity pulls the surf straight back down to the sea. As a result, pebbles move along in a zigzag known as longshore drift.

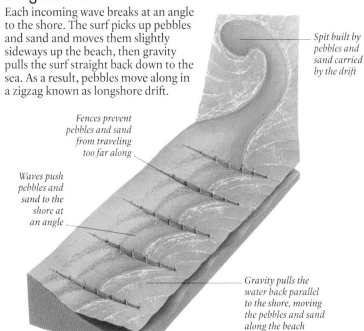

Spit built by pebbles and sand carried by the drift

Fences prevent pebbles and sand from traveling too far along

Waves push pebbles and sand to the shore at an angle

Gravity pulls the water back parallel to the shore, moving the pebbles and sand along the beach

Changing sea levels

Sea levels change continuously. Large changes took place during the Ice Age, and today changes are happening faster than ever because of climate change. In a cold phase, sea level drops as water from the oceans is locked up in glaciers. When glaciers melt, the water returns to the oceans and sea level rises.

The Dart Estuary in Devon, England, is a ria—a river valley drowned by the sea.

A dent in the land

A bay is a curved dent in the land. The waves within are usually gentle, as the headlands at either end break up the wave energy.

Chalk hills

The chalky limestone underlying rocks make a line of rolling hills farther inland.

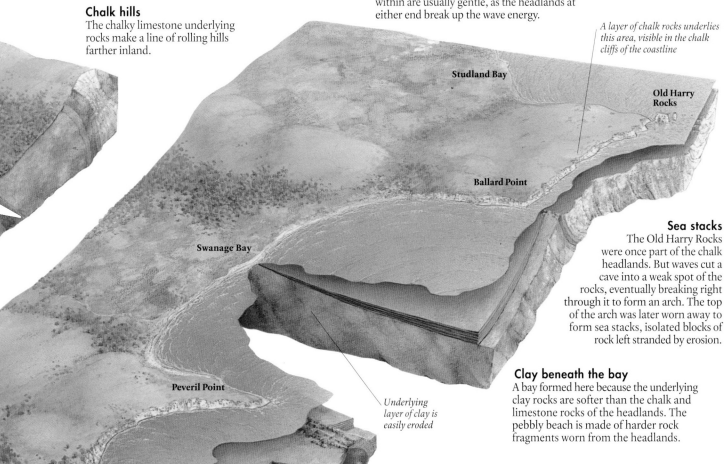

A layer of chalk rocks underlies this area, visible in the chalk cliffs of the coastline

Studland Bay

Old Harry Rocks

Ballard Point

Swanage Bay

Peveril Point

Durlston Head

Underlying layer of clay is easily eroded

Sea stacks

The Old Harry Rocks were once part of the chalk headlands. But waves cut a cave into a weak spot of the rocks, eventually breaking right through it to form an arch. The top of the arch was later worn away to form sea stacks, isolated blocks of rock left stranded by erosion.

Clay beneath the bay

A bay formed here because the underlying clay rocks are softer than the chalk and limestone rocks of the headlands. The pebbly beach is made of harder rock fragments worn from the headlands.

Headlands

The resistant limestone rocks stretching out from the coast are its headlands. These shelter the rest of the coastline, protecting softer rocks further behind. The limestone breaks up the energy of the waves, causing the water to foam in white breakers.

Sand and shingle beaches

Rocks worn from the coastline are ground down by the pounding waves to shingle or sand then eventually deposited in a bay or other sheltered area to form a beach. The sand or shingle doesn't stop moving once it is laid down—in fact, beaches may sometimes change radically within hours. In a storm, large, heavy waves break directly onto the beach. These can pick up and carry the beach material into deep water offshore, so a sandy beach can disappear overnight. The beach usually returns eventually after a long spell of calmer weather.

Underground Water

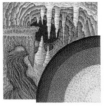

WINDING ITS WAY through tiny spaces, water slowly travels through the rocks underground. Water is found at some depth everywhere beneath the land surface. Most of this water is rain that soaked into the ground after a shower and was not immediately used up by plant roots. Some rainwater passes through the underground rocks quickly and emerges only a few hours, days, or weeks later at a spring seeping out into a river valley. Sometimes the water stays underground for many thousands of years, either because it travels a long way or because it travels slowly. During such a long time in the rocks, water usually picks up and dissolves minerals from the rocks. In this way, the water can widen cracks in the rock until eventually an enormous underground cave forms. Underground rivers run through some caves, wearing their walls away even further.

Inside the Gouffre Berger
A cross section of the Gouffre Berger is shown here. Parts of the cave have been pulled out and shown larger below.

An underground labyrinth
The Gouffre Berger is a long underground labyrinth of passageways and chambers, possibly tens of millions of years old. Its entrance is an open hole in a high limestone plateau. Today, a river runs through some parts of the cave, while others are dry. The cross sections shown on these pages reveal some of the strangely shaped rock formations built by dripping water inside the cave.

Gouffre Berger, France
The Gouffre Berger is beneath the Vercors Mountains. The limestone landscape here is honeycombed with caves and underground rivers.

The river emerges
During its passage through the cold, dark cave, the river picks up and dissolves lime and other minerals. When the river emerges, the lime-rich water forms deposits called tufa, as the bubbling spring water is warmed by the sunshine.

Walls of the cave are hollowed out by the water as it dissolves the limestone

The Canals

Hall of Thirteen

Stalagmites grow up from the floor

Rimstone pools are dammed up by a crust of minerals

Submerged river
There is running water in parts of the Gouffre Berger. The water level of the lakes and streams within caves varies rapidly. As soon as it rains outside, the caves fill up quickly.

Underground river

Rimstone pools
These steplike formations are made by a buildup of mineral deposits at the edge of a slope. Sometimes minerals are left behind as water runs over a slope. They form a crust, trapping a pool of water that overflows to form another step.

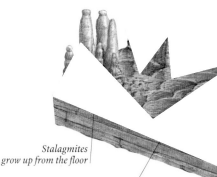

Crusts of tufa, a type of limestone

Spring water emerges from the limestone in the river valley

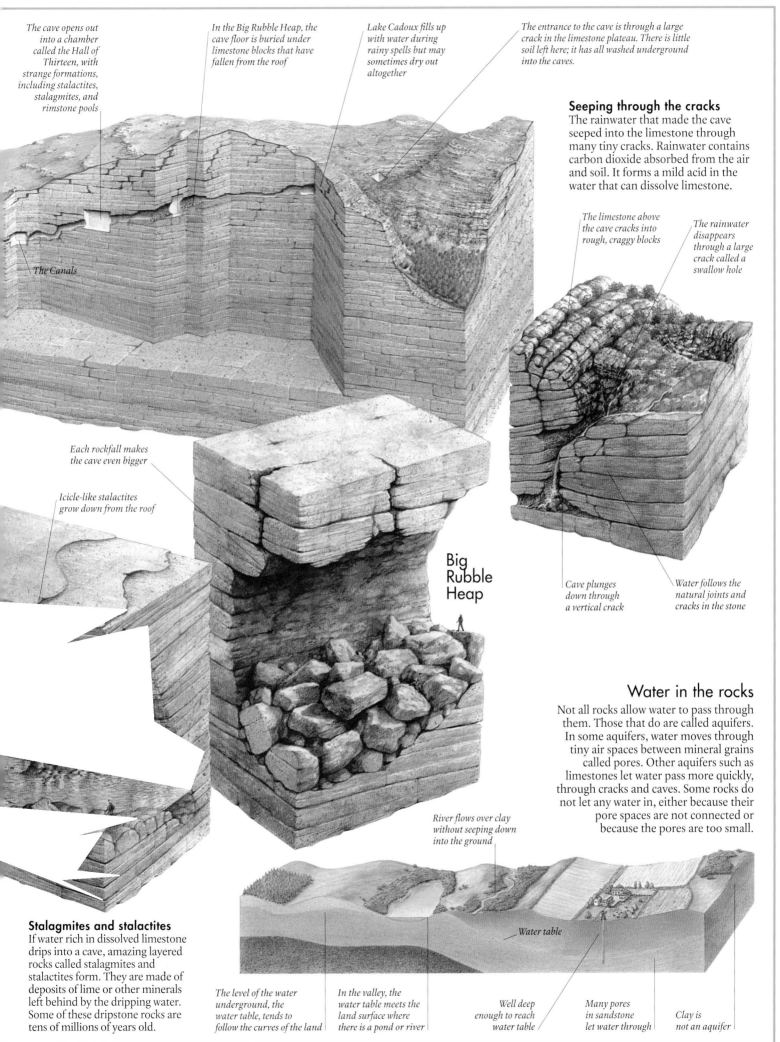

The cave opens out into a chamber called the Hall of Thirteen, with strange formations, including stalactites, stalagmites, and rimstone pools

In the Big Rubble Heap, the cave floor is buried under limestone blocks that have fallen from the roof

Lake Cadoux fills up with water during rainy spells but may sometimes dry out altogether

The entrance to the cave is through a large crack in the limestone plateau. There is little soil left here; it has all washed underground into the caves.

Seeping through the cracks

The rainwater that made the cave seeped into the limestone through many tiny cracks. Rainwater contains carbon dioxide absorbed from the air and soil. It forms a mild acid in the water that can dissolve limestone.

The Canals

The limestone above the cave cracks into rough, craggy blocks

The rainwater disappears through a large crack called a swallow hole

Each rockfall makes the cave even bigger

Icicle-like stalactites grow down from the roof

Big Rubble Heap

Cave plunges down through a vertical crack

Water follows the natural joints and cracks in the stone

Water in the rocks

Not all rocks allow water to pass through them. Those that do are called aquifers. In some aquifers, water moves through tiny air spaces between mineral grains called pores. Other aquifers such as limestones let water pass more quickly, through cracks and caves. Some rocks do not let any water in, either because their pore spaces are not connected or because the pores are too small.

River flows over clay without seeping down into the ground

Stalagmites and stalactites

If water rich in dissolved limestone drips into a cave, amazing layered rocks called stalagmites and stalactites form. They are made of deposits of lime or other minerals left behind by the dripping water. Some of these dripstone rocks are tens of millions of years old.

Water table

The level of the water underground, the water table, tends to follow the curves of the land

In the valley, the water table meets the land surface where there is a pond or river

Well deep enough to reach water table

Many pores in sandstone let water through

Clay is not an aquifer

Ice Regions

AT THE ENDS OF THE EARTH are its polar ice caps, crowning the frozen continent of Antarctica and the icy ocean of the Arctic. A vast amount of water is locked up inside the polar ice caps. The water to make this ice has come from the global oceans. Ocean water is continually evaporating as warm atmospheric air circulates. This makes moist clouds, which then drop their moisture as snow in cold or mountainous regions. This snow grows more compacted over the years and turns into glacier ice. In order to make glaciers and ice caps grow larger, the rate at which the snow falls must be much greater than the rate at which it melts so that there is snow left over at the end of each summer. Climate change is increasing the rate at which the ice is melting.

Storm waves and Arctic winds have eroded these icebergs into pinnacles. Icebergs are not made of frozen seawater. They are broken off from the end of an ice sheet or glacier so are composed of frozen fresh water.

The frozen continent

A vast ice sheet, more than 14,760 ft (4,500 m) thick in places, covers much of the frozen continent of Antarctica. The ice moves slowly outward and downhill and toward the freezing seas. On the coastline, the ice is thinner so that the summits of high mountains peek through. The sheet of ice extends out from the continental landmass, floating on the sea to form an ice shelf. At its edge, great lumps of ice split off from the main mass and float away as icebergs. Three sections of Antarctica are illustrated here.

Floating sea ice

The edge of the Antarctic ice sheet spreads out as shelves of sea ice. It floats because it is less dense than the ocean water.

Glaciers weave their way through the nunatak mountain tops

Mountains peeking through the glacier ice are called nunataks

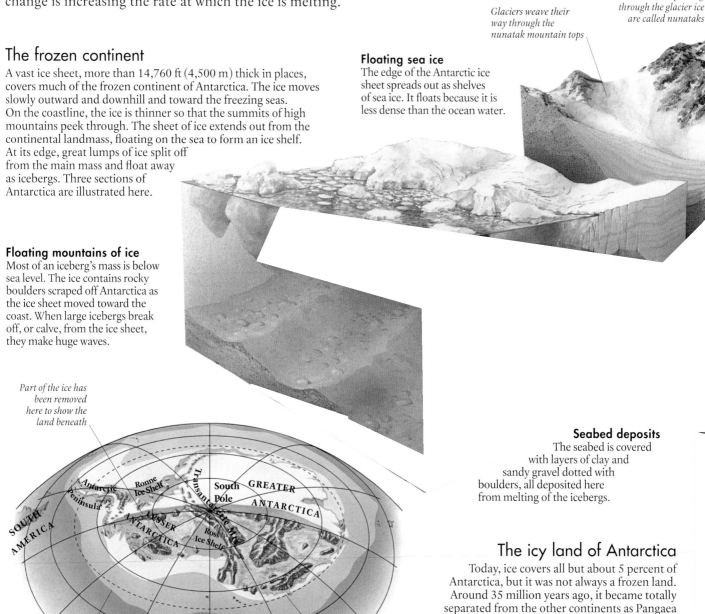

Floating mountains of ice

Most of an iceberg's mass is below sea level. The ice contains rocky boulders scraped off Antarctica as the ice sheet moved toward the coast. When large icebergs break off, or calve, from the ice sheet, they make huge waves.

Part of the ice has been removed here to show the land beneath

Seabed deposits

The seabed is covered with layers of clay and sandy gravel dotted with boulders, all deposited here from melting of the icebergs.

The icy land of Antarctica

Today, ice covers all but about 5 percent of Antarctica, but it was not always a frozen land. Around 35 million years ago, it became totally separated from the other continents as Pangaea split up. Perhaps it was then that the climate began to change. Once the cold Southern Ocean currents could circulate right round Antarctica, it was isolated from warm, tropical ocean currents. This may have been enough to trigger heavy snowfall, which led to the growth of ice sheets.

SOUTH AMERICA

Antarctic Peninsula

Ronne Ice Shelf

Transantarctic Mts.

South Pole

GREATER ANTARCTICA

LESSER ANTARCTICA

Ross Ice Shelf

SOUTH AMERICA

SOUTHERN OCEAN

The extent of the pack ice in winter

The extent of the pack ice in spring

The icy waters of the Arctic

There is no continent at the North Pole. Instead, the region includes the Arctic Ocean, the northernmost parts of North America, Europe, Asia, Greenland, and several smaller islands. The surface of the ocean is covered with salty sea ice, formed from frozen seawater. Pack ice, broken and crushed together again by the movement of the water, fringes the sea ice. About half of this pack ice melts in the summer. Glaciers crisscross the land in and near the Arctic. But in Siberia, some parts of Alaska, and Canada, there is too little snowfall for glaciers to form. The winter air is so cold that the water in the ground freezes to such a depth that it never completely thaws. This frozen ground is called permafrost.

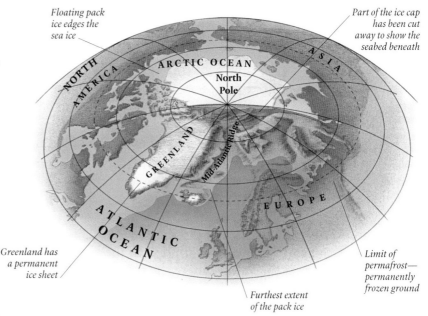

Floating pack ice edges the sea ice

Part of the ice cap has been cut away to show the seabed beneath

Greenland has a permanent ice sheet

Furthest extent of the pack ice

Limit of permafrost— permanently frozen ground

Glacier ice has scraped the mountains into rugged peaks

At the South Pole, the ice sheet is 9,000 ft (2,800 m) thick. The rocky land beneath is at about sea level.

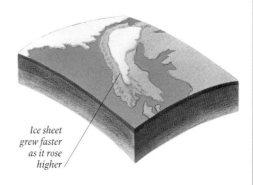

Depressed by ice

The weight of an ice sheet covering a landmass is considerable. It alters the balance of the plate, which floats on the squashy asthenosphere. As the ice sheet builds up, the asthenosphere flows out of the way and the plate sinks down. If the ice melts, the asthenosphere slowly flows back and the plate rises. These changes in land level are called isostatic changes. The sequence above shows isostatic changes created by an ice sheet over Scandinavia 30,000 years ago.

The ice sheet grows

As the ice sheet grew over Scandinavia, it spread out but also became thicker, so the surface of the ice became higher. The ice also added to the weight of the land mass, which then pressed down on the squashy asthenosphere. The ice grew thicker and higher much faster than the asthenosphere was able to sink lower out of the way.

Ice sheet grew faster as it rose higher

Frozen summits

On its way toward the sea, the ice sheet must flow around the peaks of the mountains. Because the winds are dry, they strip off and erode the upper layers of ice, revealing meteorites that fell onto the ice thousands of years ago.

Under pressure

The top of the thick ice covering Antarctica is well above sea level. But in the vast interior of the continent, the weight of the ice has pushed the rocky land below sea level. Some of the deep ice may be very old, formed by snow that fell up to a million years ago.

Asthenosphere material flows away sideways

Thick ice depresses the whole land mass

Full press

As the ice sheet reached its full extent, at last the asthenosphere caught up and flowed away. The land level became so low that the ice sheet was no longer high and cool enough to collect snow and so it began to grow smaller.

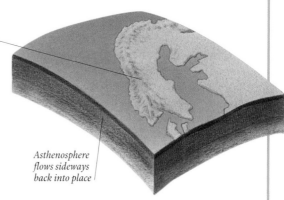

Land rebounds slowly after ice melts

Lifting land

Today, the asthenosphere is still slowly flowing back, long after the ice sheet has melted away. The plate under the Baltic Sea may eventually bounce back so much that the sea becomes dry land.

Asthenosphere flows sideways back into place

Antarctica's Ross Sea (above) is fringed by an ice shelf and littered with icebergs calved off from the main ice sheet.

Rivers of Ice

GLACIERS SNAKE DOWN THE VALLEYS of many of the world's mountain ranges. These huge masses of ice are made from layers of snow that build up until the increasing weight causes ice crystals to form. The ice becomes so thick and heavy that it starts to move—either outward in all directions, such as the vast domelike ice sheets of Greenland and Antarctica, or down a valley, such as the Athabasca Glacier seen here. Glacier ice travels slowly, less than 3 ft (1 m) a day, breaking off loose rock as it goes. At the moment, most glaciers are melting faster than new ice is forming in the high mountains. This means that glaciers are getting smaller. Glaciers have been retreating for 10,000 years.

Icy Athabasca

The Athabasca Glacier is in the Rocky Mountains of Alberta, in western Canada.

A river of melted ice runs around rocks at the snout of a glacier in Norway. The rocks have been polished smooth by rock dust that is frozen within the glacier.

The Athabasca glacier

The glacier flows out from an ice sheet, the Columbia Icefield, in the snowy mountains around the 12,293 ft (3,747 m) high Mount Columbia. The icefield was once much larger. At that time, the glaciers in the side valleys were all part of the main glacier. Today, the ice level has dropped so low that these no longer meet the main glacier. Instead, they hang isolated above the main valley. The end of the glacier is a heap of boulders and rock dust, called the terminal moraine.

This valley, carved by a glacier long ago, now "hangs" above and at the side of the main valley

The snout, or end, of the glacier is colored gray from all the rock fragments and dust in the ice

Moraine left by an earlier glacier

Glacial gravel

When glaciers advance over soft sediment, such as clay, gravel, or even dust and boulders left by a previous glacier, they smooth it into long, egg-shaped hills. These streamlined hills, called drumlins, may be up to 164 ft (50 m) high and 6,562 ft (2,000 m) long. Drumlins are usually in groups, known as a "basket of eggs" landscape.

Long side of a drumlin is parallel to the ice flow

Rock ridges

Around the edge, ridges of rock deposits are old terminal moraines, from when the glacier was longer and thicker. The gravel is now being eroded and carried away by the rivers of meltwater.

Milky rivers

Meltwater pours out from ice caves under the glacier to feed rivers. The water is milky green because it contains fine rock dust.

Lake filled with glacier meltwater is dammed up by the gravels of the terminal moraine

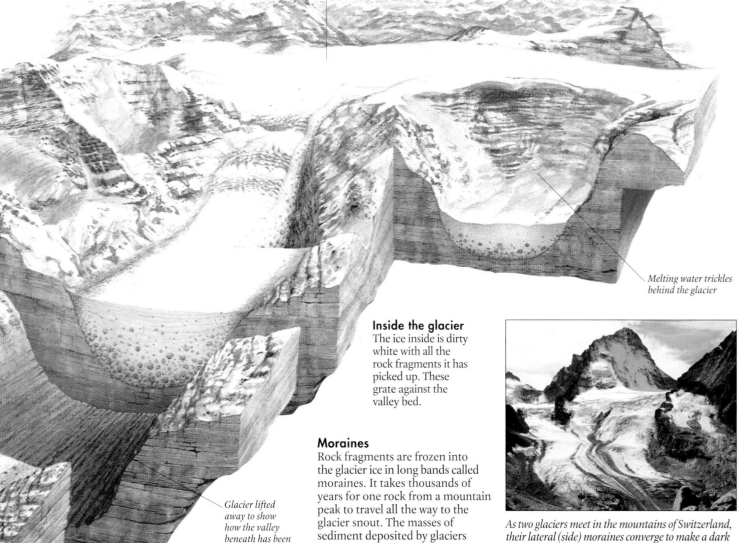

Ice on the move
When the glacier ice becomes thick enough, it starts to move under the pressure of its own weight.

Crevasses
Deep crevasses, or cracks, open up on the surface of the glacier as it travels over steep or rugged terrain.

Heavy winter snowfall "tops up" the ice dome that feeds the glacier

Steep slope
The slope at the head of a glacier is steep because the glacier has plucked rock off the mountainside.

Glued to a glacier
Melting water trickles down the rock face behind the glacier, seeping into cracks in the rock. Under the glacier, the water freezes again, "gluing" the rock on to the glacier so it can be dragged away.

Melting water trickles behind the glacier

Glacier lifted away to show how the valley beneath has been widened and gouged out to a broad U-shape

Inside the glacier
The ice inside is dirty white with all the rock fragments it has picked up. These grate against the valley bed.

Moraines
Rock fragments are frozen into the glacier ice in long bands called moraines. It takes thousands of years for one rock from a mountain peak to travel all the way to the glacier snout. The masses of sediment deposited by glaciers is also called moraines.

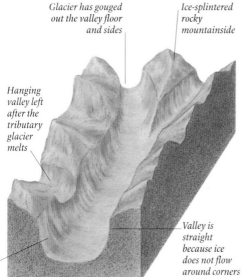

As two glaciers meet in the mountains of Switzerland, their lateral (side) moraines converge to make a dark stripe down the middle, the medial moraine. Where several glaciers meet, there are many of these stripes.

Icebreaker
The mountain surface is eroded by melting snow running into cracks in the rocks. At night, it freezes to ice, expanding and breaking apart the rock.

Polished smooth
The valley walls and floor are rasped smooth by the rocky ice, sometimes to a fine polished surface.

Glacier valleys
A glacier makes its valley wider and deeper as it carves away at the mountain sides. It scoops everything from rock fragments to huge boulders from the mountain by ice-plucking. This happens when water that seeps into cracks in the rock freezes, sticking the rock to the glacier. The resulting rock-laden ice scours the valley walls and floor as it grinds over them. Rock fragments dislodged from the steep, rocky mountain cliffs fall to the sides of the glacier and are carried away.

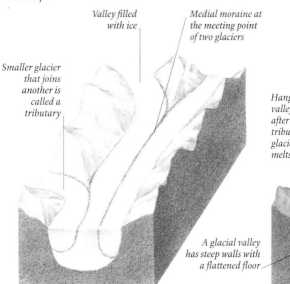

Valley filled with ice

Medial moraine at the meeting point of two glaciers

Smaller glacier that joins another is called a tributary

A glacial valley has steep walls with a flattened floor

Carving a path
Two glaciers flow together to make a larger glacier that fills the valley with ice. A smaller glacier from a valley to one side merges into the large glacier.

Glacier has gouged out the valley floor and sides

Ice-splintered rocky mountainside

Hanging valley left after the tributary glacier melts

Valley is straight because ice does not flow around corners

Empty valley
After a glacier has melted, its straight U-shaped valley is revealed. Tributary valleys hang higher above the level of the main valley.

Deserts

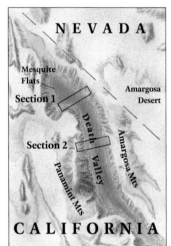

AMONG THE MOST DESOLATE places on Earth are its deserts—deserted areas where almost nothing lives. Some deserts are hot and dry all year round, others are dry with intensely cold winters, while the cold lands of the Arctic and Antarctic are also deserts. All have thin or no soils so that there is little vegetation. The sparse plant life means few creatures can survive. Less than 4 in (10 cm) of rain or snow falls each year, though years may go by when no precipitation falls at all. The dry air over the desert means that any surface water rapidly evaporates. During the rare rainstorms, there is no vegetation to slow down the running surface water. Flash floods pour into lakes that then quickly dry up, leaving behind salt flats. The Earth's desert regions are shown in this map. Rainfall is decreasing as the planet heats up due to climate change, which leads to an increase in desert land.

In the tundras of the northernmost part of North America, almost all the water is frozen beneath the surface

NORTH AMERICA

Because mountains near the Pacific coast catch all the rainfall, the air inland is dry

Death Valley

Sonoran

ATLANTIC OCEAN

Tropic of Cancer

PACIFIC OCEAN

Equator

SOUTH AMERICA

Cold ocean currents off South America cool the wind blowing on land. Any moisture makes fog at the coast—so very little reaches the Atacama Desert

Atacama

Tropic of Capricorn

This is one of the many huge playas, or dried-up lake beds, in the Atacama Desert in Chile.

Hot, dry, and low

Death Valley tops the lists of the hottest temperatures, the lightest rainfall, and the lowest elevation in the US. This inland valley is a desert because the moist winds from the Pacific Ocean drop all their rain on the mountains nearer to the coastline. There is no soil and very little vegetation. On the rare occasions when it rains, the water pours over barren rock, scouring off all loose fragments and sand. The coarse rocky material is dropped at the foot of the mountain cliffs, while sand and salty silt is spread out on the hot valley floor, where it eventually dries out. Two sections of Death Valley are illustrated below.

NEVADA

Mesquite Flats

Amargosa Desert

Section 1

Death Valley

Section 2

Amargosa Mts

Panamint Mts

CALIFORNIA

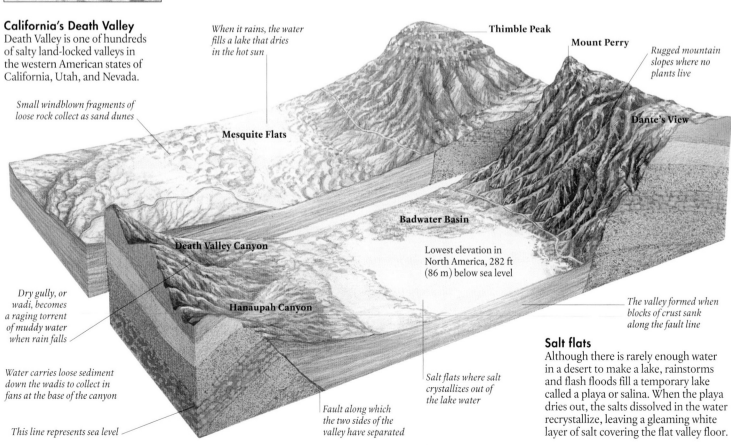

California's Death Valley
Death Valley is one of hundreds of salty land-locked valleys in the western American states of California, Utah, and Nevada.

Small windblown fragments of loose rock collect as sand dunes

When it rains, the water fills a lake that dries in the hot sun

Thimble Peak

Mount Perry

Rugged mountain slopes where no plants live

Mesquite Flats

Dante's View

Death Valley Canyon

Badwater Basin

Dry gully, or wadi, becomes a raging torrent of muddy water when rain falls

Hanaupah Canyon

Lowest elevation in North America, 282 ft (86 m) below sea level

The valley formed when blocks of crust sank along the fault line

Water carries loose sediment down the wadis to collect in fans at the base of the canyon

Salt flats where salt crystallizes out of the lake water

This line represents sea level

Fault along which the two sides of the valley have separated

Salt flats
Although there is rarely enough water in a desert to make a lake, rainstorms and flash floods fill a temporary lake called a playa or salina. When the playa dries out, the salts dissolved in the water recrystallize, leaving a gleaming white layer of salt covering the flat valley floor.

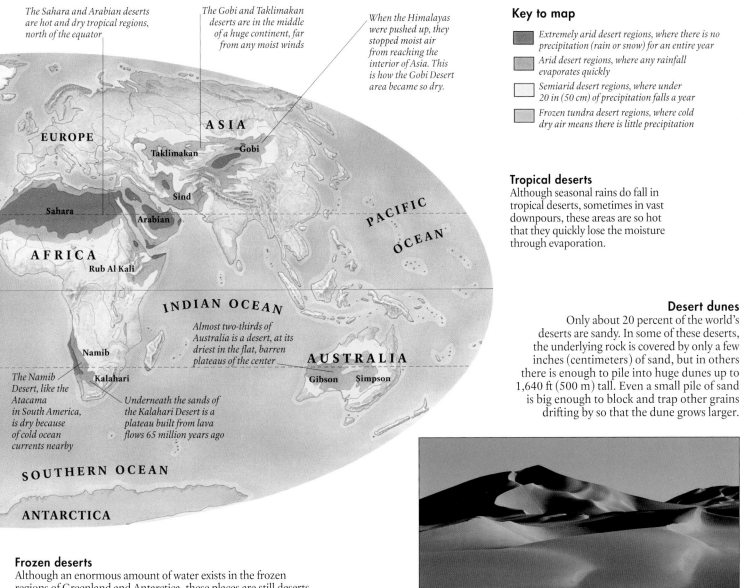

The Sahara and Arabian deserts are hot and dry tropical regions, north of the equator

The Gobi and Taklimakan deserts are in the middle of a huge continent, far from any moist winds

When the Himalayas were pushed up, they stopped moist air from reaching the interior of Asia. This is how the Gobi Desert area became so dry.

EUROPE

ASIA

Taklimakan

Gobi

Sind

Sahara

Arabian

AFRICA

Rub Al Kali

PACIFIC

OCEAN

INDIAN OCEAN

Almost two-thirds of Australia is a desert, at its driest in the flat, barren plateaus of the center

AUSTRALIA

Namib

Gibson

Simpson

The Namib Desert, like the Atacama in South America, is dry because of cold ocean currents nearby

Kalahari

Underneath the sands of the Kalahari Desert is a plateau built from lava flows 65 million years ago

SOUTHERN OCEAN

ANTARCTICA

Key to map

Extremely arid desert regions, where there is no precipitation (rain or snow) for an entire year

Arid desert regions, where any rainfall evaporates quickly

Semiarid desert regions, where under 20 in (50 cm) of precipitation falls a year

Frozen tundra desert regions, where cold dry air means there is little precipitation

Tropical deserts

Although seasonal rains do fall in tropical deserts, sometimes in vast downpours, these areas are so hot that they quickly lose the moisture through evaporation.

Desert dunes

Only about 20 percent of the world's deserts are sandy. In some of these deserts, the underlying rock is covered by only a few inches (centimeters) of sand, but in others there is enough to pile into huge dunes up to 1,640 ft (500 m) tall. Even a small pile of sand is big enough to block and trap other grains drifting by so that the dune grows larger.

Frozen deserts

Although an enormous amount of water exists in the frozen regions of Greenland and Antarctica, these places are still deserts due to their low rainfall. It sometimes rains in Greenland, but only snow falls in Antarctica—and very little. Some places here are so dry that ice evaporates in the dry wind.

These towering dunes rise above the Sahara Desert in Algeria.

DUNES

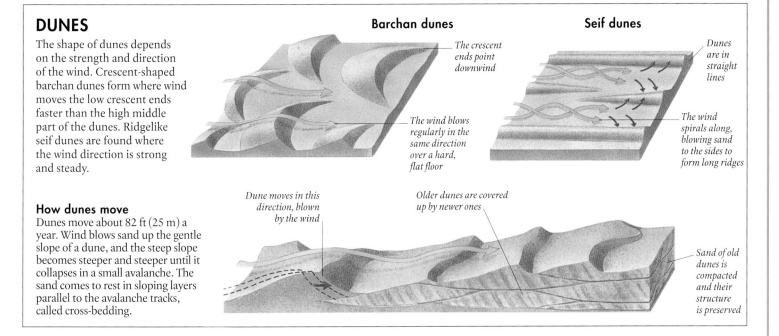

The shape of dunes depends on the strength and direction of the wind. Crescent-shaped barchan dunes form where wind moves the low crescent ends faster than the high middle part of the dunes. Ridgelike seif dunes are found where the wind direction is strong and steady.

Barchan dunes

The crescent ends point downwind

The wind blows regularly in the same direction over a hard, flat floor

Seif dunes

Dunes are in straight lines

The wind spirals along, blowing sand to the sides to form long ridges

How dunes move

Dunes move about 82 ft (25 m) a year. Wind blows sand up the gentle slope of a dune, and the steep slope becomes steeper and steeper until it collapses in a small avalanche. The sand comes to rest in sloping layers parallel to the avalanche tracks, called cross-bedding.

Dune moves in this direction, blown by the wind

Older dunes are covered up by newer ones

Sand of old dunes is compacted and their structure is preserved

Soil Supports Life

WITHOUT SOIL, there would be little life on Earth. Soil is the link between life and the rocky part of the Earth, supporting the plants that nourish people and animals. Soil is made where rocks are weathering and softening, breaking up into smaller particles, and giving up their rich store of chemicals in a form which plants can use. Soil contains mineral grains, air, and water. It is also rich in organic material, such as plant roots, fungi, beetles, and worms, as well as microorganisms such as bacteria and algae. The water and air in the soil are vital to plants. It takes a long time for a thick, nourishing soil to develop over the underlying rock.

Hillsides of the world

These soil profiles are found in three different climates: temperate, arid, and tropical. The thickness and richness of soil depends on climate and many other factors: underlying rock type, the age of the soil, the landscape, the drainage, the vegetation, and the diversity of animals living in the soil and nearby.

Left behind

Animals eat grass and browse the shrubs, but in turn, they leave behind their droppings, which fertilize the soil. Fallen leaves and twigs are also broken down into humus.

Soil profile

By digging down into the soil right through to the rock below, it is possible to see the entire profile of soil, as shown in the section pulled out of the temperate slope to the right. Soils are made up of layers known as horizons. Each horizon has its own unique physical, chemical, and biological characteristics. The topsoil layer at the surface is rich in organic material. Below this is the subsoil, penetrated by a few roots. Deeper still is a layer of weathered rock fragments and boulders worn from the solid bedrock.

Mat of plant roots in topsoil

Topsoil

The dark, rich topsoil is matted together with plant and grass roots. Topsoil contains humus—the remains of plants and animals in the process of being broken down to simpler chemicals. Bacteria and fungi within the topsoil help this happen.

Animal burrows let air into the soil and allow water to drain through

Rabbit burrow

Subsoil

There is less organic material in the subsoil. This horizon is rich in mineral particles weathered from the solid rock beneath. These minerals contribute new plant nutrients to enrich the soil above.

Humus and clay particles have large spongy surfaces that can hold and exchange plant nutrients

Bedrock

The constant weathering of the bedrock below the soil helps make the soil thicker. The basic texture of the soil depends to a great extent on the type of bedrock underlying it.

Roots penetrate into soil and make channels for air and water. These tree roots are also helping prevent soil from being washed away by heavy rain.

Air and water fill any gaps in the soil

Woody tissue being broken down into humus

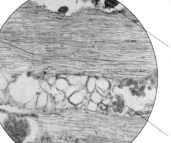

Dark brown humus

A closer look at soil

This is a section of soil viewed through a microscope. It shows the dead and decaying plant and animal material that will eventually nourish living plants growing in the soil. Air and water fill the spaces between the decaying material, along with microorganisms and tiny plants.

Droppings of the microorganism that has eaten the woody tissue

Soils on slopes

Soil continually moves downhill. When hillsides are plowed or are bare of vegetation in winter, heavy rain may wash soil into the valley below. Animals may also dislodge soil and push it slowly downhill as they walk over, or burrow through, steep slopes.

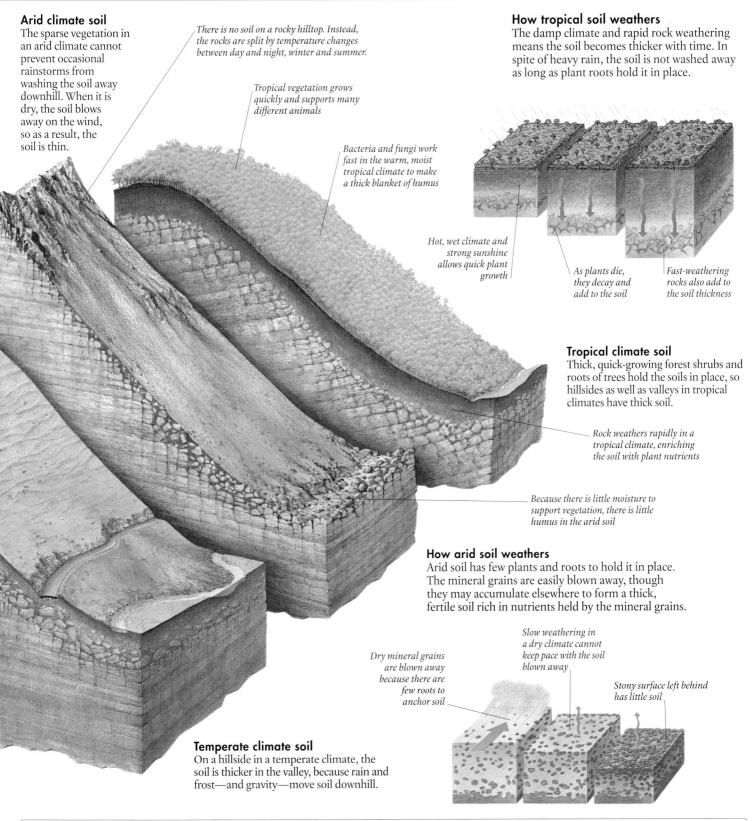

Arid climate soil
The sparse vegetation in an arid climate cannot prevent occasional rainstorms from washing the soil away downhill. When it is dry, the soil blows away on the wind, so as a result, the soil is thin.

There is no soil on a rocky hilltop. Instead, the rocks are split by temperature changes between day and night, winter and summer.

Tropical vegetation grows quickly and supports many different animals

Bacteria and fungi work fast in the warm, moist tropical climate to make a thick blanket of humus

How tropical soil weathers
The damp climate and rapid rock weathering means the soil becomes thicker with time. In spite of heavy rain, the soil is not washed away as long as plant roots hold it in place.

Hot, wet climate and strong sunshine allows quick plant growth

As plants die, they decay and add to the soil

Fast-weathering rocks also add to the soil thickness

Tropical climate soil
Thick, quick-growing forest shrubs and roots of trees hold the soils in place, so hillsides as well as valleys in tropical climates have thick soil.

Rock weathers rapidly in a tropical climate, enriching the soil with plant nutrients

Because there is little moisture to support vegetation, there is little humus in the arid soil

How arid soil weathers
Arid soil has few plants and roots to hold it in place. The mineral grains are easily blown away, though they may accumulate elsewhere to form a thick, fertile soil rich in nutrients held by the mineral grains.

Slow weathering in a dry climate cannot keep pace with the soil blown away

Dry mineral grains are blown away because there are few roots to anchor soil

Stony surface left behind has little soil

Temperate climate soil
On a hillside in a temperate climate, the soil is thicker in the valley, because rain and frost—and gravity—move soil downhill.

How soil forms
The process of soil formation in a cold climate is shown here. Glaciers strip away all soils they pass over. When they melt, new soil forms slowly from rock weathering. There is little plant and animal life to help make humus. Mosses and scrubby bushes begin the process of breaking down the bedrock. These form a network to begin to hold together a new soil.

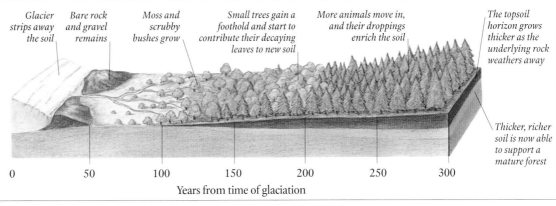

Glacier strips away the soil

Bare rock and gravel remains

Moss and scrubby bushes grow

Small trees gain a foothold and start to contribute their decaying leaves to new soil

More animals move in, and their droppings enrich the soil

The topsoil horizon grows thicker as the underlying rock weathers away

Thicker, richer soil is now able to support a mature forest

| 0 | 50 | 100 | 150 | 200 | 250 | 300 |

Years from time of glaciation

Earth's Ingredients

MILLIONS OF STARS populating the universe long ago created the ingredients of our planet. Each star was a factory for chemical elements, turning hydrogen and helium into other, heavier elements. Some stars exploded at the end of their lives, scattering their materials out through the universe. Then, 4,500 million years ago, some of this stardust clumped together to make Earth and the rest of the solar system. Since its formation, the planet Earth has shaped and regrouped the chemical elements that make it up. Its solid surface is made up of what at first seems like a bewildering variety of rocks. In fact, fewer than 10 chemical elements make up most of Earth's rocks.

Swirling white cloud patterns in the atmosphere

The solid rocky surface is seen in yellow and green

White cloud appears where the atmosphere contains masses of water droplets

The oceans are shown in blue

The eight planets and more than 200 moons condensed from the same dust cloud as the sun

Earth and its neighbors
The Earth is one of eight planets that travel around our local star, the sun, in more or less circular orbits.

Colliding in space
As the planets spin, they collide with smaller fragments. Most of these fragments were swept up in the first 1,000 million years of the solar system's history. Some remain as asteroids, and others crash onto planets as meteorites.

All life on Earth depends on the light and heat of the sun

The solar system
More than 5,000 million years ago, somewhere toward the end of one of the spiral arms of the Milky Way galaxy, a dust cloud began to gather. It was mostly made of hydrogen and helium, plus some heavier elements that were created when previous stars exploded. As the cloud became hotter and thicker, gravity pulled a clump of material toward the center, while the rest of the gas and dust flattened into a spinning disc. The central clump condensed to become the young sun. Smaller clumps of matter still spinning around the center became the planets of the solar system.

An exploding supernova shines brighter than a billion suns put together

Birth and death of stars
The most common chemical elements in the universe are hydrogen and helium. All the other chemical elements are made within stars. After a star is born, hydrogen is converted to helium in its core. When there is no more hydrogen left, the star suffers a huge collapse and begins to die. This collapse raises its temperature and brings about a synthesis of new, heavier chemical elements. Seconds later, an explosion follows, which blasts these new chemical elements out across the universe. In this way, the whole mix of about a hundred chemical elements is made.

Planet Earth

Earth's surface is unlike that of any of the other planets. Earth is surrounded by an atmosphere of gas, and nearly three-quarters of its solid surface is hidden under water. This gas atmosphere and liquid hydrosphere have separated from the solid part of the planet over thousands of millions of years. The most common element, or basic chemical, in Earth's crust is oxygen. Although oxygen is usually a gas, it is combined in the planet's rocks with the element silicon and is also present in water.

The only planet with liquid water is Earth—other planets are too hot or too cold.

Earth's atmosphere protects life on the surface from some of the harmful rays of the sun.

Relative abundance of elements

Helium 24%

Hydrogen 73.9%

Oxygen 1.04%

Carbon 0.46%

Neon 0.13%

Iron 0.11%

Nitrogen 0.1%

Silicon 0.07%

Magnesium 0.06%

Sulfur 0.04%

All other elements 0.09%

An abundance of elements

Chemical elements are basic substances that make up minerals. There are 118 elements known to science, including 89 found naturally on Earth. Some elements are much more common than others; the chart above shows the top 10 most abundant elements in our galaxy. Hydrogen is the simplest and most fundamental element from which all others are made. In the intense heat of a star, for example, hydrogen nuclei collide to make helium. When all the hydrogen is used up, the star uses its helium nuclei to make carbon and oxygen, its carbon to make magnesium, then oxygen to form silicon, and finally silicon to make iron.

Rock ingredients

Minerals, naturally formed solids with crystal structures, are made up of elements. Almost all rocks are made of silicate minerals, formed by a strong bond between the elements oxygen and silicon. Other common elements are iron, magnesium, aluminum, calcium, potassium, and sodium. This serpentinite rock is especially rich in iron and magnesium.

Serpentinite rock is made from crystals of olivine and pyroxene that have been changed by adding water into their crystal structure

Bright colors of the mineral olivine

Gray-striped crystals are feldspar minerals

Mineral mixtures

Rocks are usually made of a mixture of three or four common minerals, with a scattering of more unusual ones. The different amounts and different types of minerals present give the great variety of rocks that cover the Earth's surface. This microscopic view shows a slice of gabbro, a rock made of three main minerals, feldspar, olivine, and pyroxene, with smaller amounts of iron oxide. These minerals can be seen as individual crystals when viewed through a microscope. Most minerals are transparent when sliced thinly enough.

Black minerals are iron oxide

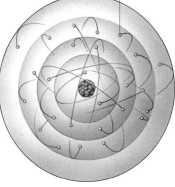

26 electrons whiz around the nucleus

Nucleus of one proton

Nucleus made of six protons and six neutrons

Six electrons round the nucleus

Structure of atoms

The smallest particle of a chemical element is an atom. Even smaller particles called protons and neutrons form the nucleus, or core, of an atom. Electrons whiz around in a cloud outside the nucleus. Each chemical element has a different number of each kind of particle. The number of protons and electrons controls which chemical elements combine with what others in order to make minerals. The atomic structures of three elements—hydrogen, carbon, and iron—are illustrated here.

Hydrogen

The most abundant element in the universe, hydrogen atoms are also the simplest, with just one proton circled by one electron. Hydrogen combines with other elements to form compounds, such as water.

Carbon

This element is made in the dying stages of a star's life. The carbon in humans, trees, and rocks all came originally from stars.

Iron

Iron is the most abundant element on Earth, but most of it is concentrated in Earth's heavy metal core. Iron is common in many minerals, and it is the chemical element that adds color to most rocks.

Igneous Rocks

WHEN PLANET EARTH first became cool enough to have a solid outer skin, igneous rocks were the first to appear on its surface. Igneous rocks are still being made today as volcanoes erupt molten magma, which cools and becomes solid. Some magma, though, does not get to the surface. Instead, it cools as igneous rock underground. Many millions of years later, the igneous rocks that cooled several miles down in the crust may become exposed at the Earth's surface by uplift and erosion. There are many different types of igneous rocks that crystallize from different magmas, under different conditions. Some are shown here, together with the minerals they contain.

Agate
The beautiful bands of agate are formed, one layer after another, as they coat the inside of gas bubbles in volcanic rock. The outermost agate layer forms first, then each layer afterward forms in time, toward the center. Sometimes there are quartz crystals lining the inner core of the agate.

Granite

If it were possible to put all the rocks of a continent in some kind of giant crushing machine, mix up the crushed rock, melt it, and then let it cool and crystallize, the result would be granite. Granite is one of the most common igneous rocks, found at the core of many mountain ranges. The first continents were made of granitelike rock. Granite contains the minerals quartz and feldspar, along with a small amount of dark minerals such as mica. Their crystals can be seen in the granite shown here: quartz is gray, different feldspars pink and white, and mica is black.

Granite

Mica
The shiny dark flakes seen in some granites are mica.

Quartz
An essential mineral in granite, quartz may be transparent but is sometimes a milky blue.

Feldspar
Igneous rocks are classified by the amount and type of feldspar they contain. Feldspar is one of the most common minerals in the Earth's crust.

Basalt

Basalt

Most of the solid surface of the Earth is made of basalt. All the solid ocean crust is basalt, and there are also many huge basalt lava flows on the continents. Basalt is formed by melting in the Earth's mantle. It is fine-grained and dark in color because of the dark minerals it contains: principally pyroxene and olivine. If basalt magma cools slowly, it grows larger crystals. Then it is called dolerite, or if the crystals are really large, gabbro.

Olivine
Olivine is a shiny green heavy mineral, rich in iron and magnesium.

This is a crystal of augite, one of the minerals in the pyroxene family, embedded in an igneous rock

Gabbro
Gabbro crystallized slowly like granite but has more dark minerals and usually no quartz.

Pyroxenes
Pyroxenes are a group of dark, dense minerals that makes up basalt, gabbro, and dolerite. They are rich in the chemical elements iron and magnesium.

Lavas

Some of the rocks formed by recrystallized lava are shown here. The texture of the rocks depends on the type of lava. Some lavas are very hot when they are erupted, spreading out quickly as they cool. Others are cooler, and move slowly, hindered by the crystals as they shape and grow.

Basalt with amygdales
Gas bubbles in lava fill up with minerals to make amygdales.

Pumice
This is a lava froth and is often part of the same eruptions as obsidian. Some pumice is so frothy and bubbly that it floats on water.

Vesicular basalt
Volcanic gas bubbles out of magma and may be trapped as the lava solidifies. The bubbles in this rock are called vesicles.

Ropy lava
The twists and turns in this rock are formed when hot flowing lava wrinkles up its cooler crust.

Pegmatite
Pegmatite contains unusually large crystals.

Volcanic bomb
Hot basalt lava cools so fast that blobs like this, which are thrown out in explosions, have solidified by the time they land on the ground.

Obsidian
This lava erupts at a low temperature, with its chemical framework already in place. This "freezes" to glassy obsidian, which has no crystals.

Gold
Some chemical elements, such as gold, do not crystallize easily as magma cools and hardens. These awkward elements get concentrated in the last bit of magma liquid and finally crystallize in cracks called veins, which open up as granite cools and shrinks.

Silver
A shiny, gray-white metal, silver is one of the few metals that crystallize from magma without combining with other chemical elements. These are called native metals; they need almost no processing before they are used.

A diamond crystallizes about 62 miles (100 km) below the surface

Diamond
Diamond is the hardest natural substance known. Its dense structure is a result of crystallizing under great pressure. It is brought to the Earth's surface in volcanic eruptions.

Galena
Galena is a sulfide of lead, which sometimes comes in large shiny crystals. Around black smokers, it makes a powdery cloud of tiny crystals.

Chalcopyrite
Most of the world's copper comes from the brassy-colored crystals of the mineral chalcopyrite. The chalcopyrite shown here is mixed with white quartz crystals.

Hematite
Hematite is an oxide of iron—iron gone rusty. Volcanic gases sometimes leave behind rich deposits of hematite. The metal iron is extracted from its red-brown crystals.

Feldspar
The dark, heavy rocks on this page contain calcium-rich feldspar. The lighter granites contain sodium- and potassium-rich feldspar.

Sulfur is scraped from volcano craters

Sulfur
These lemon yellow crystals are found around many volcanic craters and hot springs. Sometimes the sulfur is combined with other chemicals to make sulfides and sulfates.

59

Sedimentary Rocks

SEDIMENTARY ROCKS are made of sediment—particles broken up from other rocks, the hard parts of organisms, or minerals. Some of this material is created by weathering, which breaks down older rocks into fragments. These fragments are transported by wind, rivers, and glaciers and eventually deposited as layers or beds of sediment, along with any plant and animal remains trapped within. Over time, the layers are buried and squashed to become hardened, or lithified, into new rocks.

Stalactites
These hang from cave roofs when dripping water rich in dissolved limestone leaves a deposit behind.

Large, coarse pebbles   Medium-size, coarse pebbles   Small, fine pebbles   Gravel   Sand

Grains of rock

Pebbles, gravel, and sand in a riverbed or on the beach are the raw materials for new sedimentary rock. As they tumble along in the water, pebbles and rock fragments may fracture, while continuing to be chemically weathered or dissolved. Where the grains settle, they may be buried by other layers. Water that percolates through the layers sometimes contains rock material. If this should crystallize around the rock grains, it cements them together to make sedimentary rock.

Sandstone
The grains of sand that make a sandstone tell the rock's history. Those with a polished surface may be quartz grains that have been rolled around on a beach. Sand grains with a matte surface like ground glass show the sandstone was formed in a desert.

Breccia and conglomerate
A pebble beach might become hardened and lithified to make conglomerate (below). The pebbles with sand grains in between are firmly held together by a rock cement. Breccia (right) forms in the same way, but its fragments are much rougher around the edges.

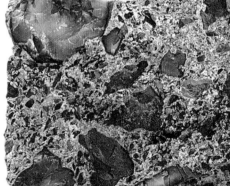

Rounded flint pebbles in this conglomerate have been smoothed by tumbling in water

Sharp rock fragments may pile up at the bottom of a cliff to form breccia

Bauxite
Bauxite is a mix of aluminum minerals left behind in tropical climates when all the other rock chemicals weather away.

Grindstone
This grindstone for grinding corn kernels was fashioned in Roman times. The rough surface texture of the conglomerate, made of flint pebbles, is perfect for the job.

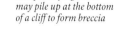

The metal aluminum, used in foil, is extracted from bauxite

Limestone

It is easy to see grains of sand on a beach that might one day become sandstone, but limestone's chemicals are transported invisibly—they are dissolved in water. Sea creatures and plants take carbon dioxide from sea water. This changes the chemical balance of the water, and as a result, the chemicals that make limestone—calcium and magnesium carbonate—separate from the water. They are deposited in thick layers of limy mud on the seabed to make limestone.

Clay

Tiny clay grains weathered from other rocks travel suspended in water. These are what makes river water look muddy. When river water meets the sea, the clay flakes flock together into mud (left), which may form mudstone, clay stone, or shale.

Sharp-edged flint arrowhead

Shelly limestone

Sea creatures such as shellfish help make limestone by taking dissolved calcium carbonate from the water to make their shells. When the shellfish die, they sink into the limy ooze on the sea- or lake bed and help build up limestone.

Flint

Flint (above) is fine-grained silica, the same chemical as quartz. Flint breaks to make sharp edges so was ideal for making knives and arrowheads.

Chalk

Chalk is a soft, pure limestone. Europe's chalk cliffs are made from the skeletons of tiny floating plants that lived in the sea more than 65 million years ago.

Sharp edges of halite crystals

The gypsum crystals in a desert rose grow in flakes that resemble rose petals

Rock salt

When the sea or salty desert lakes evaporate, they leave salt, which hardens to become rock. Halite is one of the salts that makes up the rock.

Desert rose

When underground water in the desert evaporates, it leaves behind salts such as gypsum to crystallize. These gypsum crystals wrap around grains of sand.

Metamorphic Rocks

METAMORPHIC ROCKS ARE MADE from preexisting igneous, sedimentary, or other metamorphic rocks. As plates in Earth's crust move together, the rocks within are stretched, squeezed, heated—and changed. A rock's minerals recrystallize and its original texture changes. Usually these changes happen deep inside the Earth's crust, where it is hot enough and there is enough pressure from the overlying rocks to make rocks recrystallize without melting. The recrystallization creates new crystals and different minerals. The rocks may also become folded or crushed, so they get a new texture in which all the mineral grains are aligned according to the pressures on the rock.

Limestone to marble

Intense heat changes limestone into marble, an even-grained, sugary-textured rock. Most limestones contain some chemicals other than calcium carbonate. These may be caught in the limestone as grains of sand, or wisps of clay. When the calcium carbonate recrystallizes to marble, it reacts with these other chemicals to make new metamorphic minerals, which come in many colors. The colored minerals may be in layers that become folded by the pressures of metamorphism.

Limestone
Muddy gray limestone can be transformed into the multicolored marbles seen here.

Marble streaked with green

White marble
White marble from southern Spain is recrystallized from a pure calcium carbonate limestone.

White marble, made from pure calcium carbonate limestone, was used to build the Taj Mahal in Agra in northern India. This monument is decorated in fine patterns with colored slivers of marble and precious stones inlaid in the white.

Granite becomes gneiss

When granite is metamorphosed, the original crystals that make it up recrystallize. If metamorphism is not very intense, the new rock still looks like granite, but it takes on a new texture if there is also directional pressure, like the squeezing that happens in a mountain range. The new rock, gneiss, has a foliated texture. This means the minerals form wispy, more or less parallel bands.

Granite
This igneous rock is made of quartz, feldspar, and mica crystals. These are all more or less the same size and are randomly scattered about the rock.

Gneiss
Heat and pressure change granite to gneiss. Gneiss shows dark wispy bands of mica curling around creamy white knots of feldspar.

Migmatite
This rock formed in heat so intense that parts of it melted. Migmatite shows no sign of the texture of the original rock, which might have been granite. Its banding has been intricately folded.

Banded gneiss
The stripy bands of this rock show that directional pressure was high when it recrystallized.

Gemstones

Rocks are sometimes soaked with watery fluid during metamorphism. This helps recrystallization so that bigger, clearer crystals grow. Many of the crystals shown here can be cut and polished as gemstones.

Only deep green beryl crystals like this can be called emeralds

Ruby is colored a rich red by chromium chemicals

Sapphire is the same family as ruby but is deep blue

Beryl has the same chemical composition as emerald

Jade

Jade minerals are tough, making them suitable for gemstones. They come from the metamorphism of dark igneous rocks and are often found in fault zones. There are two types: nephrite and jadeite.

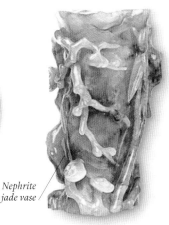

Nephrite jade boulder from New Zealand formed in the high pressure of the Alpine Fault

Nephrite jade vase

Jadeite jade cut stones

Garnets

Garnets are a group of minerals found in metamorphic rocks. Garnet forms crystals that come in many different colors. Their color depends on the chemistry of the original rock. Almandine, for example, gets its rich brownish-red color from iron. Garnet is a dense, hard mineral, tough enough to be used as an abrasive for grinding and polishing.

Almandine

Pyrope

Demantoid

Hessonite

Quartzite

When a sandstone that is made entirely of quartz sand grains is metamorphosed, each grain of sand grows to a different shape in response to increased pressure. The once-rounded sand grains interlock and the spaces between are filled with quartz to form a tough new metamorphic rock, quartzite.

Phyllite

The mica crystals within phyllite give it a shiny look.

Black slate

Cubes of brassy-colored pyrite dot this rock.

Garnet schist

This schist grows garnet crystals in response to higher heat and pressure.

Gray mudstone

This is a sedimentary rock formed in seas or lakes.

Mudstone to schist

A dull, gray mudstone can be transformed by metamorphism into sparkling, colored, crystalline rocks. At different temperatures and pressures, different new minerals appear. The rocks here are shown in a sequence from left to right. The rocks on the left have been formed at the lowest temperatures and pressures, and those on the right, at the highest.

Kyanite schist

Its pale blue crystals formed in the depth and heat of a mountain range.

INDEX

ACKNOWLEDGMENTS

The author would like to acknowledge the help and advice of the following people and organizations: British Antarctic Survey; Simon Conway-Morris at Cambridge University; Rob Kemp at Royal Holloway, University of London; Martin Litherland at the British Geological Survey; Ian Mercer at the Gemmological Association; Ron Roberts; Robin Sanderson.

Picture Credits
a=above; b=below/bottom; c=center; f=far; l=left; r=right; t=top

The publisher would like to thank the following for their kind permission to reproduce the photographs:

Alamy Stock Photo: John Cancalosi 12bl, Hemis 53crb, LatitudeStock 26clb, Neil Porter 28clb, View Stock 48tr, World Travel Collection 49bl, Worldwide Picture Library 34bc, 35bl; **Alberta Geological Survey:** 24cla; **Dorling Kindersley:** Natural History Museum 10cr, Natural History Museum, London 10ca, 10c, 10cb, 58tr, 58cra, 58c, 58cr, 58crb, 58bc, 59cl, 59cr, 59cb, 59bl, 59bc, 60tc, 60tr, 60ca, 60br (Foil), 61cla, 61br, 62ca, 62cra, 62cl, 63tc, 63tr, 63ca, 63cra, 63cl, 63cl (Garnet Stone), 63c, 63cr, 63cb, 63cb (Mica Schist); **Dreamstime.com:** Monica Furlong 62c, Njnightsky 8bl, Pancaketom 10cb (Fern

Fossil), Pstedrak 51cr, Kseniya Ragozina 52cr, Scaliger 5tr, Valeriy Tretyakov 50cl; **Getty Images:** Cedric Favero 43c, Gavin Hellier / robertharding 45cra, Matt Ottosen ~ Ottosen Photography 32tr, Zhouyousifang / Moment 30cla, Planet Observer / Universal Images Group 5tc; **Komando Kroketa "https://www.komandokroketa.org/":** 34c; **NASA:** MODIS Land Rapid Response Team, NASA GSFC 39cr; **NASA's Earth Observatory:** Lauren Dauphin 25tr; **Science Photo Library:** Jean-Loup Charmet 6bl, Mda Information Systems 19tr, NASA 39c, David Parker 8br, Uc Regents, Natl. Information Service For Earthquake Engineering 23tr, Dirk Wiersma 57cb, Jessica Wilson / USGS 5br (Two images); **Shutterstock.com:** Islamic Footage 21tr, OpMaN 54clb, PhotoVisions 7cra

Additional photography on pages 56 to 63 by: Andreas Einsiedel, Colin Keates, and Harry Taylor of the Natural History Museum, and Tim Ridley Every effort has been made to trace the copyright holders, and we apologize for any unintentional omissions. We would be pleased to insert the appropriate acknowledgment in any subsequent edition of this publication.

All other images © Dorling Kindersley

Great pictorial atlases from DK

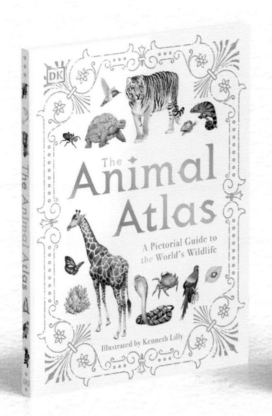

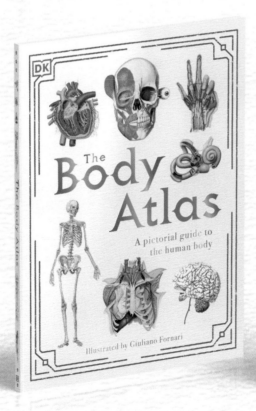

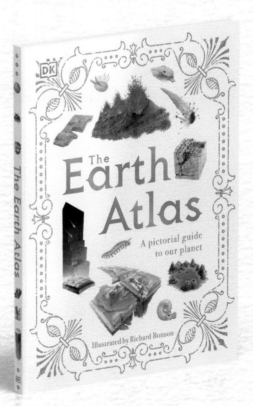